The
Emergence
of
American
Political Issues

The West Series in Journalism

Consulting Editors:

Everette Dennis,
Arnold Ismach
and Donald Gillmor

The Emergence of American Political Issues: The Agenda-Setting Function of the Press

Donald L. Shaw
Maxwell E. McCombs

In Association With

Lee B. Becker
Cynthia Long Clemmer
L. Edward Mullins

Thomas A. Bowers
Mary Elizabeth Junck
Eugene F. Shaw

David H. Weaver

WEST PUBLISHING CO.
St. Paul • New York • Boston
Los Angeles • San Francisco

1977

Copyright © 1977 By WEST PUBLISHING CO.
　　　　　　　　50 West Kellogg Boulevard
　　　　　　　　P.O. Box 3526
　　　　　　　　St. Paul, Minnesota 55165

Library of Congress Cataloging in Publication Data

Shaw, Donald Lewis.

　The emergence of American political issues.

　Bibliography: p.
　Includes index.
　1.　Journalism—Political aspects—United States.
I.　McCombs, Maxwell E., joint author.　II.　Title.

PN4888.P6S5　　　070.4'3　　　77–23766

ISBN 0–8299–0142–6

Preface

This book is an outgrowth of an ongoing research program which initially was associated with the University of North Carolina School of Journalism. It is now also identified with the Communication Research Center of the S. I. Newhouse School of Public Communication at Syracuse University and several other university research centers around the country.

This research program basically seeks to determine more precisely the relationships between the American press and the society it serves. By hypothesizing that there is an "agenda-setting" function of the press, we have sought to discover what press audiences actually learn, and the conditions under which they learn, from the daily barrage of press information. This type of research focuses on cognitive variables rather than on changes in attitudes, which is another form of research that flourished between 1940 and 1965. Walter Lippmann in his classic 1922 book, *Public Opinion*, commented that the press daily fills in our mental picture of the distant world—he called it our "unseen" environment—and we are only now trying to find out how this filling-in takes place.

The first agenda-setting study was done by the senior authors of this book using a panel of undecided Chapel Hill voters in the 1968 Presidential campaign. That study suggested that voters do in fact learn from what they read or view, and that voters do not read only about candidates and issues they favor while avoiding information about those they do not favor. That initial study was published by *Public Opinion Quarterly* under the title, "The Agenda-Setting Function of Mass Media.["]

As a next step in the exploration of agenda-setting, we conducted a larger panel study in Charlotte, N.C., during the 1972 Presidential campaign which resulted in the basic data reported here. With the exception of Lee Becker of Ohio State University, all authors of this book at one time or another had a connection with the University of North Carolina School of Journalism either as a faculty member or graduate student. In 1973 Maxwell McCombs left UNC to head the Communication Research Center at the S. I. Newhouse School of Public Communication, Syracuse University, and over time several other members of the Charlotte research team shifted to other places. This shifting of university affiliation by McCombs and other research team members necessarily caused delays in completion of this study. Since the time this project actually began with a series of planning workshops in the fall 1971, the field of agenda-setting research has grown considerably with research papers and articles by a variety of authors appearing fairly regularly. In fall 1974 Syracuse University sponsored a national conference on the findings of agenda-setting research and more than 60 scholars from political science, journalism and communications, and other fields attended. Several of these conference papers were published in the Spring 1976 issue of the *Journal of Communication*. Nevertheless, this book represents the first integrated treatment of the agenda-setting function of the press, and it is the first book-length treatment of the subject.

While *The Emergence of American Political Issues* is based upon a 1972 data set, it especially aims to incorporate some of the more recent research findings and to draw some tentative conclusions for the general as well as the scholarly reader. Like all scholarly findings, these conclusions will be amplified and changed over the years as our research experience deepens.

The book is designed to discuss agenda-setting from four points of view. Chapters 1 and 2 focus on defining agenda-setting as a concept and discuss its broad implications within the community setting. Chapters 3 through 5 discuss the potentially competing issue agendas which are available to voters from the news itself (Chapter 3), from advertising (Chapter 4), or from discussion with other people (Chapter 5). Chapter 6 compares the long-term effects on voter learning resulting from either reading about the campaign in the newspaper or viewing it on television. Chapters 7 through 9 look at agenda-setting from the point of view of the audience to discover what kinds of people are "susceptible" to agenda-setting influence or under what kinds of conditions voters are likely to learn about issues and candidates from the press. Finally, Chapter 10 discusses agenda-setting within the larger political process. Methodological details, including the study questionnaires, are included in an appendix.

There are many to whom we owe thanks. Included are the University of North Carolina which provided a Research Council Grant, and the National Association of Broadcasters and E. W. Scripps Company which provided grants at the start of the project. The Rockefeller Foundation funded a full-time position for the project, and we were able to hire communication specialist Charles Spellman to direct actual field work. The Syracuse Communication Research Center provided help of many kinds, from typing support to data analysis for various authors.

There were many graduate or undergraduate students who helped in one way or another with data gathering, coding, or analysis. We particularly thank Garry Ballance and Ernest Boykin, then UNC undergraduates, and Cindy Long Clemmer, then a UNC graduate student, for help with coding and data analysis. From Syracuse University, Eleanor Branning, Sandy Miller, and Meg Bartschi deserve our special thanks.

Mary Elizabeth Junck, a UNC graduate and now Sales Development Manager for the Miami *Herald* and Miami *News*, was a research specialist for the Charlotte *News* and the

Observer when the study was conducted, and she greatly assisted us by setting up training sessions for interviewers. The Charlotte papers also made their facilities available to us for a field headquarters. To all these people—and others we do not have room to mention—we owe our sincere thanks.

Donald L. Shaw

Maxwell E. McCombs

NOTES

[1]Maxwell E. McCombs and Donald L. Shaw, "The Agenda-Setting Function of Mass Media," *Public Opinion Quarterly*, 36: 176-87 (Summer 1972).

Contents

The
Emergence
of
American
Political Issues

†

The Agenda-Setting Function of the Press

MAXWELL E. McCOMBS
Syracuse University

DONALD L. SHAW
University of North Carolina at Chapel Hill

All I know is just what I read in the papers.

Will Rogers

We Americans cherish the notion that America is a land firmly based upon laws, not men, and that political choices are made within the arena of competing ideas and issues. Voters carefully weigh both candidates and issues in making political choices. Few of us, however, have direct access to candidates.

We learn from our friends and from the press, newspapers, television, magazines, radio. In a nation in which the average person spends nearly three hours a day viewing television and another half hour reading a newspaper—to mention only two media—it is not surprising that we sometimes ask if the press, or "mass media," to use the term of many, does not do more than merely relay news between candidates and voters.

Does the press not actually create political and social issues by news choices made day after day? Publicity is at least potential power. Historian Daniel Boorstin has pointed out that it has become possible to achieve widespread (if not always long-lasting) fame merely by appearing in the national press, particularly television. You can become famous, so to speak, by becoming well known! Can this be true of political candidates or issues?

We are quite aware the press daily brings us news information. We may be less conscious of the way this news over time may add up to shape our ideas about important issues or personalities. Political leaders certainly are aware of the role of the press in campaigns. They usually adapt to the practices and prejudices of the press.

In 1968 Richard Nixon did what many would have regarded as impossible only a few years earlier. He returned from the politically dead to become President in an election squeaker. It was, some said, a "new" Nixon, or as political reporter Joe McGinness put it more simply, a Nixon more able to understand, or use, the press. Mr. Nixon was more approachable. On occasion he even smiled at reporters. He was seen in a bathrobe. Mr. Nixon was—the reporters themselves had to admit it—human. By a close vote he won over Senator Hubert Humphrey.

By 1972, President Nixon won re-election over Democratic Senator George McGovern with one of the largest majorities in history. When it came to voting, those whom President Nixon from time to time had loosely referred to as the silent majority were noisy enough. In that campaign, President Nixon spent only a small amount of time on the campaign trail. Instead he used a carefully constructed media campaign which emphasized selected issues and urged voters to re-elect the President.

Through press news, comment, and advertising, information about issues and personalities spreads throughout the land. But our suspicion remains: does the press merely relay information? Is it only a transmission belt? Or, by exercising conscious and unconscious choice, does the press not have the ability to spotlight certain issues for a short while, hammer away at others over time, and simply ignore still others? This book examines that agenda-setting power of the press, the hypothesis that the press itself has some power to establish an agenda of political issues which both candidates and voters come to regard as important.

The Popular View

Certainly in the popular view mass communication exerts tremendous influence over human affairs. The ability of television, newspapers, magazines, movies, radio, and a whole host of new communications technologies to mold the public mind and significantly influence the flow of history is a widely ascribed power. In the political arena, candidates spend substantial sums for the services of image-makers—a new kind of mass communication artist and technocrat who presumably works magic on the voters via the mass media.

Early social scientists shared with historians, politicians, and the general public a belief in the ability of mass communication to achieve significant, perhaps staggering, social and political effects. But beginning with the benchmark Erie County survey conducted during the 1940 presidential campaign,[1] precise, quantitative research on the effects of mass communication in election campaigns, public information campaigns, and on numerous public attitudes soon gave the academic world a jaundiced view of the power of mass communication. From a theory of massive communication effects—most everyone's view in 1940—the academic world moved 180 degrees in less than two decades. Summing up the first two decades of empirical mass communication research, Joseph Klapper in 1960 listed two major conclusions in his book, *The Effects of Mass Communication:*

1. Mass communication ordinarily does not serve as a necessary and sufficient cause of audience effects, but

rather functions among and through a nexus of mediating factors and influences.

2. These mediating factors are such that they typically render mass communication a contributory agent, but not the sole cause, in a process of reinforcing the existing conditions. . . .[2]

We moved from an all-powerful 1984 view to the *law of minimal consequences,* a notion that the media had almost no effect, in two decades! But despite the "law," interest in mass communication has proliferated during the past 15 years. Political practitioners, especially, continue to emphasize the use of mass communication in election campaigns.[3] Surely all this is not due simply to cultural lag in spreading the word about the law of minimal consequences. Rather it is because *mass communication does in fact play a significant political role.* This is not to say that the early research was wrong. It simply was limited. To gain precision, science must probe carefully circumscribed areas. Unfortunately, the early research on mass communication concentrated on attitude change. Given the popular assumption of mass media effects, it was not a surprising choice. But the chain of effects that result from exposure to mass communication has a number of links preceding attitude and opinion change. In sequence, the effects of exposure to communication are generally catalogued as:

Awareness→Information→Attitudes→Behavior

Early research chose as its strategy a broad flanking movement striking far along this chain of events. But as the evidence showed, the direct effects of mass communication on attitudes and behavior are minimal. Klapper's summary which reflects the law of minimal consequences is quite correct in its conclusion about the effects of mass communication on attitudes and opinions. So in recent years scholars interested in mass communication have concentrated on earlier points in the communication process: awareness and information. Here the research has been most fruitful in documenting significant social effects resulting from exposure to mass communication. People do learn from mass communication.

Not only do they learn factual information about public affairs and what is happening in the world, they also learn how much importance to attach to an issue or topic from the emphasis placed on it by the mass media. Considerable evidence has accumulated that editors and broadcasters play an important part in shaping our social reality as they go about their day-to-day task of choosing and displaying news. In reports both prior to and during political campaigns, the news media to a considerable degree determine the important issues. In other words, the media set the "agenda" for the campaign.

This impact of the mass media—the ability to effect cognitive change among individuals, to structure their thinking—has been labeled the *agenda-setting function of mass communication*. Here may lie the most important effect of mass communication, its ability to mentally order and organize our world for us. In short, the mass media may not be successful in telling us what to think, but they are stunningly successful in telling us what to think *about*.[4]

Assertions of Agenda-Setting

The general notion of agenda-setting—the ability of the media to influence the salience of events in the public mind—has been part of our political culture for at least half a century. Recall that the opening chapter of Walter Lippmann's 1922 book *Public Opinion* is titled: "The World Outside and the Pictures in Our Heads." As Lippmann pointed out, it is, of course, the mass media which dominate in the creation of these pictures of public affairs.[5]

More recently this assumption of media power has been asserted by presidential observer Theodore White in *The Making of the President, 1972.*

> The power of the press in America is a primordial one. It sets the agenda of public discussion; and this sweeping political power is unrestrained by any law. It determines what people will talk and think about—an authority that in other nations is reserved for tyrants, priests, parties and mandarins.[6]

The press does more than bring these issues to a level of political awareness among the public. The idea of agenda-setting asserts that the priorities of the press to some degree become the priorities of the public. What the press emphasizes is in turn emphasized privately and publicly by the audiences of the press. As political scientist Robert Lane has suggested:

> The common viewing, listening, and reading patterns of a large portion of the public tend, I believe, to set for the nation some common foci of attention, some common agendas of discussion. A reference to an issue or to a presentation of an issue is likely, in most social sets, to meet with recognition because of the overlapping exposure patterns of the members of these sets. Of course, people have different private and group agendas and these make for varied arenas of discourse, but the tendency of the media to homogenize sets means the variation is reduced, and the national agenda develops a meaningful cross-set audience and dialogue.[7]

Cognitive Effects
of Mass Communication

This concept of an agenda-setting function of the press redirects our attention to the cognitive aspects of mass communication, to attention, awareness, and information. While there was justification for earlier emphasis on attitude change,[8] it was precisely that emphasis on the affective aspects of mass communication that led to the law of minimal consequences. However, the history of mass communication research from the 1940 Erie County study to the present decade can be viewed as a movement away from short-range effects on attitudes and toward long-range effects on cognitions.[9]

Attitudes concern our feelings of being for or against a political position or figure. *Cognition* concerns our knowledge and beliefs about political objects. The agenda-setting function of mass communication clearly falls in this new tradition of cognitive outcomes of mass communication. Perhaps more than any other aspect of our environment, the political arena—all those issues and persons about whom we hold opinions and knowledge—is a secondhand reality. Especially in national politics, we have little personal or direct contact. Our knowledge comes primarily from the mass media. For the most part, we know only those aspects of national politics considered newsworthy enough for transmission through the mass media.

Even television's technological ability to make us spectators for significant political events does not eliminate the secondhand nature of our political cognitions. Television news is edited reality just as print news is an edited version of reality. And even on those rare occasions when events are presented in their entirety, the television experience is not the same as the eyewitness experience.[10]

Our knowledge of political affairs is based on a tiny sample of the real political world. That real world shrinks as the news media decide what to cover and which aspects to transmit in their reports, and as audiences decide to which news messages they will attend.

Yet, as Lippmann pointed out, our political responses are made to that tiny replica of the real world, the *pseudoenvironment*, which we have fabricated and assembled almost wholly from mass media materials. The concept of agenda-setting emphasizes one very important aspect of this pseudoenvironment, the *salience* or amount of emphasis accorded the various political elements and issues vying for public attention.

Many commentators have observed that there is an agenda-setting function of the press and Lippmann long ago eloquently described the necessary connection between mass communication and individual political cognitions. But like much of our folk wisdom about politics and human behavior, it was not put to empirical test by researchers for over half a century.

Empirical Evidence of Agenda-Setting

The first empirical attempt at verification of the agenda-setting function of the mass media was carried out by McCombs and Shaw during the 1968 U.S. presidential election.[11] Among undecided voters in Chapel Hill, North Carolina there were substantial correlations between the political issues emphasized in the news media and what the voters regarded as the key issues in that election. The voters' beliefs about what were the major issues facing the country reflected the composite of the press coverage, even though the three presidential contenders in 1968 placed widely divergent emphasis on the issues. This suggests that voters—at least undecided voters—pay some attention to all the political news in the press regardless of whether it is about or originated with a favored candidate. This contradicts the concepts of selective exposure and selective perception, ideas which are central to the law of minimal consequences. Selective exposure and selective perception suggest that persons attend most closely to information which they find congenial and supportive.

In fact, further analysis of the 1968 Chapel Hill survey showed that among those undecided voters with leanings toward one of the three candidates, there was less agreement with the news agenda based on their preferred candidate's statements than with the news agenda based on all three candidates.

While the 1968 Chapel Hill study was the first empirical investigation based specifically on agenda-setting, there is other scholarly evidence in the mass communication/political behavior literature which can be interpreted in agenda-setting terms. Let's briefly consider several examples.

The first example comes from the 1948 Elmira study, research which cemented the strong role of interpersonal rather than mass communication in the election process. For an optimum view of the agenda-setting influence of the press, one should examine those Elmira voters with minimal interpersonal contact. As Berelson, Lazarsfeld, and McPhee noted:

> ... about one-fifth of our sample did not know the politics of any of their three closest friends in August. Such people have so little political content in their normal social interaction that what little they do learn about politics is largely independent of their social surroundings most of the time. Therefore, they are more likely than their fellows to be 'blown about' by the political winds of the times, in a way especially independent of their social surroundings.[12]

In other words, for those voters the political agenda suggested by the media is not mediated, interpreted, or confronted by interpersonal sources of influence. These voters would seem especially open to the agenda-setting influence of the press.

And the influence was there. These Elmira voters moved with the trend of the times more than did the other voters. Like the national Democratic trend that mounted during the 1948 campaign, these Elmira voters moved rapidly into the Democratic column. The cues were there in the media for all. But persons without the conservative brake of interpersonal contacts moved most rapidly with the national trend reported in the media.

The second example of agenda-setting comes from a study of county voting patterns in an Iowa referendum.[13] In this example it is easy to see the agenda-setting effects of both mass media and interpersonal news sources.

The question before the voters was calling a constitutional convention to reapportion legislative districts. Since large counties stood to gain and small counties to lose from reapportionment, the study anticipated a strong correlation between county population and proportion of votes in favor of the convention. In short, it was hypothesized that counties would vote their self-interest. And, overall, this was strikingly the case. Across all counties, the correlation is +.87 between county population and vote.

But now let us consider whether this pattern is facilitated by the presence of agenda-setting institutions. Two sources of heightened awareness were considered: a citizens' committee in favor of the convention and a daily newspaper in the county.

In the 41 counties where the citizens' committee was active, the correlation was +.92 between vote and population. In the 58 counties without such a group, the correlation was only +.59. Similar findings are reported for the presence or absence of a local daily newspaper. In the 38 counties with a local daily, the correlation was +.92. In the 61 counties without a daily, the correlation was only +.56.

Each agenda-setting source made a considerable difference in the outcome. What about their combined impact? In 28 counties with both a local daily and a citizens' committee the correlation was +.92. Where only one of these sources was present, the correlation declined to +.40; and when neither agenda-setter was present, the correlation declined to +.21.

Self-interest may have motivated many voters. But unless the issue was high on the agenda—placed there via the newspaper and local citizens' committee—this motivation simply did not come into play.

A similar "necessary condition" role for agenda-setting is found in a study of the distribution of knowledge among populations.[14] Generally, there is a knowledge gap between social classes concerning topics of public affairs, typically documented by a rather substantial correlation between level of education and knowledge of public affairs. That is to say, as level of education increases, so does the amount of knowledge about public affairs. But as communication scientist Phillip Tichenor and his colleagues discovered, the strength of this correlation, at least for some topics, is a direct function of the amount of media coverage. They found a monotonic relationship between media coverage and the strength of the education/knowledge correlation. The more the press covers a topic, the more an audience—especially audience members with more education—learn.

The Concept
of Agenda-Setting

Agenda-setting not only asserts a positive relationship between what various communication media emphasize and what voters come to regard as important, it also considers this influence as an inevitable by-product of the normal flow of news.

Each day editors and news directors—the gate-keepers in news media systems—must decide which items to pass and which to reject. Furthermore, the items passed through the gate are not treated equally when presented to the audience. Some are used at length, others severely cut. Some are lead-off items on a newscast. Others follow much later. Newspapers clearly state the value they place on the salience of an item through headline size and placement within the newspaper—anywhere from the lead item on page one to placement at the bottom of a column on page 66.

Agenda-setting asserts that audiences learn these saliences from the news media, incorporating a similar set of weights into their personal agendas. Even though these saliences are largely a by-product of journalism practice and tradition, they nevertheless are attributes of the messages transmitted to the audience. And as the idea of agenda-setting asserts, they are among the most important message attributes transmitted to the audience.

This notion of the agenda-setting function of the mass media is a relational concept specifying a strong positive relationship between the emphases of mass communication and the salience of these topics to the individuals in the audience. This concept is stated in causal terms: increased salience of a topic or issue in the mass media influences (causes) the salience of that topic or issue among the public.

Agenda-setting as a concept is not limited to the correspondence between salience of topics for the media and the audience. We can also consider the saliency of various attributes of these objects (topics, issues, persons, or whatever) reported in the media. To what extent is our view of an object shaped or influenced by the picture sketched in the media, especially by those attributes which the media deem newsworthy? Some have argued, for example, that our views of city councils as institutions are directly influenced by press reporting with the result that these local governing groups are perceived to have more expertise and authority than they actually possess.[15]

Consideration of agenda-setting in terms of the salience of both topics and their attributes allows the concept of agenda-setting to subsume many similar ideas presented in the past. The concepts of status-conferral, stereotyping, and image-making all deal with the salience of objects or attributes. And research on all three have linked these manipulations of salience to the mass media.

Status-conferral, the basic notion of press agentry in the Hollywood sense, describes the ability of the media to influence the prominence of an individual (object) in the public eye.

On the other hand, the concept of stereotyping concerns the prominence of attributes: All Scots are thrifty! All Frenchmen are romantic! Stereotyping has been criticized as invalid characterization of objects because of its overemphasis on a few selected traits. And the media repeatedly have been criticized for their perpetuation of stereotypes, most recently of female roles in our society.

The concept of image-making, now part of our political campaign jargon, covers the manipulation of the salience of both objects and attributes. A political image-maker is concerned with increasing public familiarity with his candidate (status-conferral) and/or increasing the perceived prominence of certain candidate attributes.

In all cases, we are dealing with the basic question of agenda-setting research: How does press coverage influence our perception of objects and their attributes?

Issue Salience
and Voting

Political issues have become salient as a factor in voter behavior in recent years. The importance of party identification, long the dominant variable in analysis of voter decisions, has been reduced. This stems both from a conceptual rethinking of voter behavior and from an empirical trend.

The role of party identification as the major predictor of how a voter would cast his presidential ballot now appears to be an empirical generalization limited to the 1940s and 1950s. By the 1960s whatever underlying conditions that gave rise to this dominance appear to have shifted and significant declines in the predictive and explanatory power of party identification begin to appear on the empirical record.[16]

Conceptually, issues also began to play a greater role in the analysis of voter decision-making. In 1960 the Michigan Survey Research Center, whose earlier work has provided much of the evidence for the key role of party identification, added a new set of open-ended questions to its interview schedule seeking information about the voter's own issue concerns—that is, those issues which were salient to the individual voter—and the perceived link between those issues and the parties.

Analysis of these questions reveals a major role for issue salience in the presidential vote decision. For example, in predicting voting choice in 1964 the weights were .39 for candidate image, .27 for party identification, and .23 for issues. (Each weight controls for the influence of the two other factors.) While candidate image had the greatest weight in 1964 (a plausible outcome with Lyndon Johnson and Barry Goldwater, who were associated with extreme positions, as the contenders), issues also had a strong effect.[17] As political scientist David RePass notes, "The remarkable thing that emerges from this analysis is that *salient issues had almost as much weight as party identification in predicting voting choice.*"[18] And, as if in anticipation of the findings from research on the agenda-setting function of the mass media, he also noted that while it was not easy to predict exactly which issues would be salient in a particular election, "the public does seem to respond most to current and recurring news and events."[19]

The 1968 Comparative State Election Project (CSEP), conducted by the Institute for Research in Social Science at the University of North Carolina, also gave issues a major conceptual role in the analysis.[20] CSEP examined the "distance" between each voter's attitude and the position of each presidential candidate. Both for the state voter cohorts and nationally, issue proximity was a more powerful predictor of presidential vote than party identification. While explicit attempts to weight the issues for personal salience to the voter failed to enhance their predictive strength, Beardsley[21] feels that this is a methodological artifact.

In 1972 issues took center stage. Summing up its analysis of that election, the Survey Research Center concluded: "Ideology and issue voting in that election provide a means for better explaining the unique elements of the contest than do social characteristics, the candidates, the events of the campaign, political alienation, cultural orientations, or partisan identification."[22]

Voters do respond to the issues. The new evidence on the impact of issues appearing in the late 1960s and early 1970s provided empirical vindication for V. O. Key, Jr.'s view that "voters are not fools." Key had long contended that voters in fact responded to the issues and to the events creating and surrounding those issues.[23] Again, anticipating the concept of an agenda-setting function of the press operating across time to define political reality, Key argued that the "impact of events from the inauguration of an administration to the onset of the next presidential campaign may affect far more voters than the fireworks of the campaign itself."[24] Even the benchmark Erie County survey found that events between 1936 and 1940 changed more than twice as many votes as did the 1940 presidential campaign itself.

It is, of course, the press that largely structures voters' perceptions of political reality. As we shall see, the press can exert considerable influence on which issues make up the agenda for any particular election. Not only can the press influence the nature of the political arena in which a campaign is conducted but, on occasion, it can define (albeit inadvertently) an agenda which accrues to the benefit of one party. To a considerable degree the art of politics in a democracy is the art of determining which issue dimensions are of major interest to the public or can be made salient in order to win public support.

In 1952 the Republicans, led by Dwight Eisenhower, successfully exploited the three "K's"—Korea, Corruption, and Communism—in order to regain the White House after a hiatus of twenty years. The prominence of those three issues, cultivated by press reports extending over many months and accented by partisan campaign advertising, worked against the incumbent Democratic party. Nor is 1952 an isolated example. One of the major campaign techniques discussed by political analyst Stanley Kelley in *Professional Public Relations and Political Power* is nothing more than increasing the salience of an issue that works to an incumbent's disadvantage.[25]

These are what social scientist Angus Campbell and his colleagues[26] call *valence issues* in contrast to our usual consideration of *position issues* on which voters take various pro or con stances. A valence issue is simply a proposition, condition, or belief that is positively or negatively valued by all the voters. At least two, if not all three, of the 1952 K's were valence is-

sues. No one was for crime or corruption. When valence issues
are the case it is simply a matter of where the credit or blame
is to be assigned. Apparently in 1952 enough voters assigned
the blame to the Democrats to win the election for the Republicans. To the extent that the press (via its agenda-setting function) has a direct impact on the outcome of a particular election, it is likely to be through the medium of valence issues
which directly accrue to the advantage or disadvantage of one
political party. But, as we shall see, that is only one facet of the
agenda-setting function of mass communication.

NOTES

[1]Paul Lazarsfeld, Bernard Berelson, and Hazel Gaudet, *The People's
Choice* (New York: Columbia University Press, 1948).

[2]Joseph Klapper, *The Effects of Mass Communication* (Glencoe: The
Free Press, 1960), p. 8.

[3]Ray Hiebert, Robert Jones, John Lorenz, and Ernest Lotito (eds.), *The
Political Image Merchants: Strategies in the New Politics* (Washington: Acropolis Books, 1971).

[4]See Bernard C. Cohen, *The Press and Foreign Policy* (Princeton:
Princeton University Press, 1963) p. 13; also Lee Becker, Maxwell
McCombs, and Jack McLeod, "The Development of Political Cogni-
tions," in Steven H. Chaffee (ed.), *Political Communication*, Vol. 4,
Sage Annual Reviews of Communication Research (Beverly Hills:
Sage Publications, 1975), pp. 21–63.

[5]Walter Lippmann, *Public Opinion* (New York: Macmillan, 1922).

[6]Theodore White, *The Making of the President, 1972* (New York: Bantam, 1973), p. 327.

[7]Robert E. Lane, "Alienation, Protest and Rootless Politics in the
Seventies," in Hiebert, Jones, Lorenz, and Lotito, *op. cit.*, pp.
286–87.

[8]Maxwell McCombs and Thomas Bowers, "Television's Effects on Political Behavior," in George Comstock *et al.*, *The Fifth Season: How TV Influences the Ways People Behave* (Santa Monica: Rand Corporation, in press.)

[9]Maxwell McCombs, "Mass Communication in Political Campaigns: Information, Gratification, and Persuasion," in F. Gerald Kline and Phillip J. Tichenor (eds.), *Current Perspectives in Mass Communication Research*, Vol. 1, Sage Annual Reviews of Communication Research (Beverly Hills: Sage Publications, 1972).

[10]Kurt Lang and Gladys Engel Lang, *Politics and Television* (Chicago: Quadrangle, 1968).

[11]Maxwell E. McCombs and Donald L. Shaw, "The Agenda-Setting Function of Mass Media," *Public Opinion Quarterly*, 36:176–87 (Summer 1972).

[12]Bernard Berelson, Paul Lazarsfeld, and William McPhee, *Voting* (Chicago: University of Chicago Press, 1954), pp. 138–39.

[13]David Arnold and David Gold, "The Facilitation Effect of Social Environment," *Public Opinion Quarterly*, 28:513–16 (Fall 1964).

[14]G. A. Donohue, Phillip J. Tichenor and C. N. Olien, "Mass Media and the Knowledge Gap: A Hypothesis Reconsidered," *Communication Research*, 2:3–23 (January 1975).

[15]David L. Paletz, Peggy Reichert, and Barbara McIntyre, "How the Media Support Local Governmental Authority," *Public Opinion Quarterly*, 35:80–92 (Spring 1971).

[16]Edward C. Dreyer, "Media Use and Electoral Choices: Some Political Consequences of Information Exposure," *Public Opinion Quarterly*, 35:544–53 (Winter 1971–72); also Walter D. Burnham, "The End of American Party Politics," *Transaction*, 7:12–22 (December 1969).

[17]David E. RePass, "Issue Salience and Party Choice," *American Political Science Review*, 65:389–400 (June 1971).

[18]*Ibid.*, p. 400.

[19]*Ibid.*, p. 393.

[20]David M. Kovenock, James W. Prothro, and Associates (eds.), *Explaining the Vote* (Chapel Hill: Institute for Research in Social Science, 1973).

[21]Philip L. Beardsley, "The Methodology of the Electoral Analysis: Models and Measurement," in Kovenock, Prothro, and Associates (eds.), *op. cit.*, p. 43.

[22]A. H. Miller, W. E. Miller, A. S. Raine, and T. A. Brown, "A Majority Party in Disarray: Policy Polorization in the 1972 Election," Mimeographed report, University of Michigan.

[23]V. O. Key, Jr., *The Responsible Electorate* (New York: Vintage Books, 1966).

[24]*Ibid.*, p. 9.

[25]Stanley Kelley, *Professional Public Relations and Political Power* (Baltimore: Johns Hopkins Press, 1956).

[26]Angus Campbell, Philip E. Converse, Warren E. Miller, and Donald E. Stokes, *Elections and the Political Order* (New York: John Wiley and Sons, 1966), p. 170.

2 The Press Agenda in a Community Setting

DONALD L. SHAW
University of North Carolina at Chapel Hill

> To say that editors attach relative significance to particular for-
> eign policy stories—indeed, to all stories—and thus tell their
> readers what to think about, is to say that the reader adapts to his
> newspaper, so that he knows how to receive signals about impor-
> tance or salience, and how to interpret them.
>
> Bernard C. Cohen, The Press and Foreign Policy

Harold Lasswell has compared the press to the body's nervous
system, granting to the press the power of providing early
warning of danger or pain and tying the body's many functions
together as a coherent system.[1] This analogy suggests an important point about the relationship between the press and
public it serves. The press and public are parts of an integrated social system which, to survive, must develop the ability
to cope with social problems. Societies which cannot solve
their problems cannot survive.

Before we can deal with our social, political, and economic
problems, however, we must become aware of them. They must

become part of the agenda of public issues. The process may be quick. A major earthquake creates an immediate social and economic problem of which we very soon become aware. But an inequity in income tax laws or a need to change a public education policy may not.

The agenda-setting power of the press may be thought of as a process of consensus building between those who have access to the press or whom the press regularly covers with news, the press itself, and the audience or society at large. Agenda-setting represents social learning.

Crucial Variables in the Agenda-Setting Process

Figure 2-1 demonstrates several important variables in the agenda-setting process. This chapter briefly discusses them and relates how the chapters which follow focus on important elements in this total process.

Agenda-setting describes a complex array of variables. Broadly speaking, half of the array involves the news media—the kinds of events reporters decide to cover or the amount of emphasis they decide to put upon them—and the other half involves the audience. Is the audience interested? Do people have a chance to see the evening television news? Agenda-setting is the end result of a process of institutional and personal decisions, whether we are talking about political issues or issues unrelated to any political campaign.

Events/Issues

There is no firm consensus among reporters regarding the definition of an "event" or "issue." A car wreck in which five people are killed is a discrete and important event, particu-

FIGURE 2-1

Crucial Variables in the Agenda-Setting Process

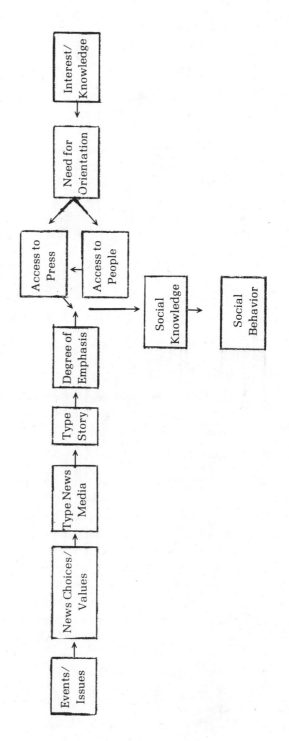
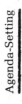

larly if one of the passengers is a state governor. A press conference by the President is an event, even though the timing
and length of the conference are carefully prearranged. But is
the press coverage of unemployment of minority groups in your
town an event or issue worth focusing upon day-after-day?
Would this unemployment become an important event or issue
if the President decided to open his press conference on this
topic? The world is full of events and issues. The press cannot
cover all of them. It necessarily must be selective.

News Choices/Values

Reporters are self-conscious about their community information role. Through either academic or on-the-job training (or
both), they become socialized to many cues about what is or is
not legitimate news. News media and newsrooms differ. Lasswell has pointed out that one of the main jobs of the press is to
"survey" the community.[2] Most reporters would agree, although they would simply think of this as covering the local
news.

Confronted with an infinite choice of events about which,
theoretically, one can write news stories, reporters soon learn
to differentiate "real" events from those not worth covering.
Reporters learn from their news editors, who themselves were
once reporters and who continue to learn from those above
them. And, as Timothy Crouse has vividly described,[3] reporters
learn from each other. They look at the same events, share the
same news norms, and race against the same deadlines, although such news media as magazines of course have longer
deadlines.

In a sense, although it has not been studied very systematically, reporters themselves apparently have an agenda-building or consensus-sharing process. And not all news media were
created equal. Such newspapers as the New York *Times* and
Washington *Post* and the major networks apparently have a

disproportionate power to shape the agenda for other reporters. While there is plenty of room for reporters to write about events that other reporters do not cover—and some reporters look for these events—there is always the risk that your fellow reporters will suspect that you do not have a very sound news sense; otherwise you would be covering what everyone else does.

While this process sounds circular, and it certainly is, one must keep in mind it does insure that we are forced to focus on some issues in common merely because our reporters and editors agree upon the news. Balanced against our natural concern that we are getting enough diverse viewpoints to make intelligent political choices we must realize that a certain amount of agreement provides a chance for social intercourse and stability. It is difficult to hear or read about too many things at once. Chapter Three in this study shows that in fact the news media are often in agreement about major political agenda items. If reporters and editors agree, are we not likely to?

Type News Media

While Chapter Three shows the news media to be in substantial agreement on the topics emphasized during a political campaign, we remain aware that the audiences of television news and newspapers may be quite different. Those with more education or reading skills naturally find the going easier with newspapers.[4] Furthermore, even the same people may bring different moods and expectations to the same news media at different times. Sometimes we seek information, sometimes we avoid it. Sometimes we are merely passive. We are not totally predictable.

Successful communication requires an attending audience. But the degree of that attention can shape the success of press messages. Television is tightly constrained by time. News must be really important to be presented on a television news special. Otherwise it must be trimmed to fit the time space. Less constrained by space, newspapers can present information in greater detail and cover it regularly over a longer period of time.

Chapters Three and Six find that these time and space constraints differentiate between the ability of television and newspapers to convey a news agenda to voters. Television appears to have an immediate but short-range effect, especially as the campaign comes to a close, while newspapers have a slower, but longer-lasting effect. The tortoise appears to come very close to overtaking the hare.

Type Story

While we often think of using the press to catch up with the news, we just as often use the press for diversion by reading features or watching situation comedies. We also learn commercial information—how can we avoid it!

It is likely that our agenda of important social and political issues somehow results from the mixture of all kinds of press content that we absorb, as well as all the nonpress kinds of information we learn, such as from our friends and family. In our minds, news flows into commercials into feature stories. Most likely our minds synthesize diverse information into a coherent picture of the campaign so that we can vote as the campaign comes to an end. The montage becomes a picture.

Chapters Three and Four discuss how differences in news choices which determine where certain types of information are displayed in a newspaper (Vietnam news was heavily displayed on the front page, for example, while education news rarely was) can influence voters, and how issues emphasized . on television commercials reach voters. The placement of news, as well as what news is covered, is an important variable in the agenda-setting process.

Degree of Emphasis

While reporters have some measure of power to determine what events they will write about, news editors have the power to determine what stories will be selected, where they will be displayed, and how long in time or space they will be carried. Journalists commonly assume that longer, front page stories are more important than shorter, inside stories. Agenda-setting hypothesizes that the news audience learns to take news importance from these placement cues.

Such power lies in the copypencils of news editors, yet several studies have shown that news editors, like reporters, are constrained in their judgments.[5] They are influenced by what competing newspapers are carrying or what is coming in over the wire services. That the wire services carry a type of news story argues strongly that a particular item is important news. While not necessarily meaning to, the national wire services have consensus-building power and can influence news norms.

While reporters are influenced by people they often know personally, news editors are influenced by other news editors up the line whom they probably do not know but upon whose news judgment they have learned to depend and trust.

Chapter Six examines the audience learning from issues emphasized over a long period by newspapers and over a shorter period by television news. The result appears to be that the longer the newspaper emphasis over time (up to about two months), the more likely voters will come to agree that a particular news issue is important. When it comes to issues, voters are not interested in a flash in the pan.

Interest/Knowledge

If many choices and judgments lie behind the finished news report, the message will not succeed unless the audience is in a position to read or hear it. Figure 1 isolates several important variables, but additional variables could be added and no doubt will be as agenda-setting research continues.

Behavioral scientists are fond of asking chicken-and-egg questions. Does political knowledge lead to political interest and then to news exposure? If you answer yes, then someone is bound to pounce on you, asking where did the knowledge come from first?

While these questions are important, in agenda-setting research we necessarily must begin with the present level of voter interest and/or knowledge and then see how this relates to information seeking. One scholar has argued that the press may so overinform us on some issues that we simply substitute reading and viewing for action.[6] While reading and viewing definitely constitute important political behavior, they most certainly do not substitute for voting. Chapter Eight explores this relationship and finds some limited evidence that some voters *may* substitute news exposure for political action.

Need for Orientation

Some political commentators have identified a new issue-oriented voter emerging during the past two decades,[7] a voter far less likely to vote the straight Republican or Democratic ticket than did his parents.[8] If true, voters with high political interest and low amounts of political information should feel a need for orientation.[9]

In Chapter Seven, David Weaver divides voters into groups according to this orientational need. He found considerable evidence that the greater this need, the greater the press exposure, and learning from the press. In Chapter Nine, L. Edward Mullins discusses the same situation for young voters and Lee Becker, in Chapter Eight, finds that particular issues may be disproportionately influential in determining what we learn from a campaign.

Access to the Press &
Access to Other People

Voters, of course, must have access to informational sources, whether press or other people. Chapter Five shows that voters engage in information seeking or sharing with others as the campaign comes to an end. We long have been aware of the important role which is played by other people in keeping us informed or providing us with opinions.[10] Our friends and the groups to which we belong can provide issue agendas alternative to those of the press. Or they may merely supplement those of the press. One would expect those who are socially isolated to be more influenced by the press—there are fewer competing agendas—than those who belong to groups and Chapter Nine does find some evidence of this among young voters.

Likewise, if the press is to have an influence, we must have access to it. No doubt that is one reason why dictatorships move to suppress a free press. The press can provide an alternative agenda to one supported by the government. Powerful competing agendas are disruptive of a political system and political systems strive for stability. Two scholars in recent years have pointed out that even in comparatively free Western society, the press can expect to experience pressures when it is too critical, particularly in times of great social tension.[11] Yet even suppression or control of the press likely will not be able to stop the rise of at least an underground press or interpersonal agenda of issues, such as occurred in Russia in recent years.

While agenda-setting can be thought of as a sociological process from the point of view of society at large, or as a psychological process from the point of view of the individual voter who wants to learn about issues or personalities, it also can be influenced abruptly by the political system.

Agenda-Setting, Social Learning
& Social Behavior

Agenda-setting therefore really stands for a complex, interrelated set of processes. Here we have argued that one can think of agenda-setting as society's way of arriving at a consensus of important issues. But really, as indicated earlier, there likely are institutional agenda-setting processes (by information sharing among reporters and news editors, for example) which are nested within the larger societal process.

From another point of view, agenda-setting indexes social learning and it is this learning by voters that is the central focus of this book.

Many groups in our society, of course, are concerned with shaping the agenda. Public relations is a whole field devoted to shaping the agenda from one point of view. Through organized action, pressure groups attempt to put their messages before the public, often by attracting press coverage.[12] The press, important as it may be, represents only one important link in this agenda-setting process.

While the Charlotte study attempts to fill some of the gaps in our knowledge of this process, investigation has only begun. We need better knowledge of not only what are the pertinent components in the process but how all the components fit together. As a conceptual puzzle, most of the pieces are still missing.

Those of us in agenda-setting research suspect that somehow this label indexes something more significant than the label indicates. Here we have speculated about a consensus-building process at the societal level. We have called it social learning. We have emphasized audience as much as press. While the growing evidence of agenda-setting is in bits and pieces from this and other studies in the expanding field of agenda-setting research, some tentative conclusions are emerging about the effects of different news media and news treatments on audiences.

We always have known the press is a messenger but we are just beginning to obtain a glimpse of how that messenger himself can shape the message and, perhaps, in a small and largely unconscious way help shape our common social destiny. That glimpse, of course, is the major challenge of agenda-setting research.

Research Strategies in Charting the Agenda-Setting Process

Agenda-setting research necessarily brings together results of two methodological approaches: content analysis and field survey. As yet agenda-setting research has not produced any tightly controlled experimental studies, although this certainly will come in time.

The study location we selected was Charlotte, North Carolina, a metropolitan city located some distance from the press influence of other metropolitan centers. This simplified the content analysis task by enabling the study to concentrate upon one major newspaper, the Charlotte *Observer* (the most widely-read newspaper in Charlotte) and on the three evening television network broadcasts.

To determine whether voters actually learn about events and issues from the press, we selected several important campaign issues, including news about the Vietnam War and governmental corruption, to follow throughout the entire 1972 campaign year in the *Observer* and at selected times during the campaign on network news. These issues are described in the methodological appendix.

The study included interviews with a panel of Charlotte voters in June and October (in person) and in November just after the election (by telephone). The panel ranged in size from 254 to 421, with 227 interviewed across all three interview waves. Each survey interview sought to chart changing voter views toward issues and candidates. Some questions were open-ended and others asked voters to rank issues. We attempted to control for panel effects and discover normal media usage and demographic data. The questionnaires and study strategy are detailed in the appendix.

NOTES

[1]See Harold D. Lasswell, "The Structure and Function of Communication in Society," in Wilbur Schramm (ed.), *Mass Communications* (Urbana: University of Illinois Press, 1960), pp. 117–130.

[2]*Ibid.*

[3]See Timothy Crouse, *The Boys on the Bus* (New York: Ballantine Books, 1972).

[4]See Bruce H. Westley and Werner J. Severin, "A Profile of the Daily Newspaper Non-Reader," *Journalism Quarterly*, 41: 45–50, 156 (Winter 1964); and Jeanne Penrose *et al.*, "The Newspaper Non-reader 10 Years Later: A Partial Replication of Westley-Severin," *Journalism Quarterly*, 51: 631–38 (Winter 1974).

[5]Many of these studies are cited in Donald L. Shaw, "Surveillance vs. Constraint: Press Coverage of a Social Issue," *Journalism Quarterly*, 46:707–12 (Winter 1969).

[6]See Paul F. Lazarsfeld and Robert K. Merton, "Mass Communication, Popular Taste and Organized Social Action," in Lyman Bryson (ed.), *The Communication of Ideas* (New York: Institute for Religious and Social Studies, 1948), pp. 95–118.

[7]See Walter DeVries and V. Lance Tarrance Jr., *The Ticket-Splitter: A New Force in American Politics* (Grand Rapids, Mich.: William B. Eerdmans Publishing Co., 1972); and V. O. Key, Jr., *The Responsible Electorate: Rationality in Presidential Voting, 1936–1960* (Cambridge, Mass.: Harvard University Press, 1966).

[8]See Paul F. Lazarsfeld, Bernard Berelson, and Hazel Gaudet, *The People's Choice* (New York: Columbia University Press, 1948); Bernard R. Berelson, Paul F. Lazarsfeld, and William N. McPhee, *Vot-*

ing: *A Study of Opinion Formation in a Presidential Campaign* (Chicago: University of Chicago Press, 1954); and Angus Campbell *et al.*, *The American Voter* (New York: Wiley, 1960).

[9]See Maxwell E. McCombs, "Editorial Endorsements: A Study of Influence," *Journalism Quarterly*, 44: 545–48 (Fall 1967).

[10]Many studies could be cited but see Elihu Katz and Paul F. Lazarsfeld, *Personal Influence* (Glencoe, Illinois: Free Press, 1955).

[11]See Fredrick S. Siebert, *Freedom of the Press in England 1476-1776* (Urbana, Illinois: University of Illinois Press, 1952); and John D. Stevens, "Freedom of Expression: New Dimensions," in Ronald T. Farrar and John D. Stevens (eds.), *Mass Media and the National Experience* (New York: Harper & Row, 1971), pp. 14–37.

[12]See Roger W. Cobb and Charles D. Elder, *Participation in American Politics: The Dynamics of Agenda-Building* (Boston: Allyn and Bacon, 1972).

*

News and the Public Response

DONALD L. SHAW
University of North Carolina at Chapel Hill

CYNTHIA LONG CLEMMER
University of North Carolina at Chapel Hill

> *Universally it is admitted that the press is the chief means of contact with the unseen environment. And practically everywhere it is assumed that the press should do spontaneously for us what primitive democracy imagined each of us could do spontaneously for himself, that every day and twice a day it will present us with a true picture of all the outer world in which we are interested.*
>
> Walter Lippmann, *Public Opinion*

Successful communication obviously involves both a message sender and a receiver. In America we expect to be deluged with hundreds of press messages every day from our car radios or tapes, newspapers, magazines, or television. The very ubiquity of press messages makes it easy to deemphasize the role of the individual reader, listener, or viewer. With so much sound and fury, can we fail to learn? We can if we do not listen or read. Yet who wants to be a hermit? So we pick and choose.

Successful political communication depends upon our collec-
tive willingness to attune ourselves to the press or other
sources of information, or at least not to avoid them.

At the same time, the news we see and hear about is the result of many decisions. While God may indeed allow events to
happen, reporters do not always choose to write about them,
nor do news editors, columnists, editors, or publishers. Reporters can be as choosy as readers but they also share many
news norms with others in the news process. An event goes
through many gates to become a polished news report.

This chapter discusses how issues rise and fall from the
press agenda and the response made by the public to this shifting agenda.

In general the topics and issues in the Charlotte Observer
were consistently emphasized throughout the entire year
studied (see Table 3–1). Vietnam news, while accounting for
about one story of every five during the election month, never
fell lower than 15 percent of the news and editorial coverage.
The same consistency can be seen in coverage of race relations; youth, drugs, and morals; and crime, law, and order.
This consistency is not surprising in light of professional norms
regarding news values which pervade journalism.[1] The consistency also reflects the tendency for news media—the electronic
media as well as newspapers—to place heavy reliance on the
convenient, dependable wire service news.[2]

Hard pressed news editors grow accustomed to pulling information from the Associated Press and United Press International wires to fill their news space and keep local audiences
informed about events beyond their own community. Because
there is no convenient way to check out wire service reports of
events, news editors not only depend upon the speed of the
services but also upon their accuracy. In a highly readable account of the 1972 presidential campaign reporting, Timothy
Crouse makes frequent mention of the "clout" which wire service reports have back at the home office over even a newspaper's own correspondent on the scene with a candidate.[3]
Correspondents, Crouse reports, learned to dread the call-

Table 3-1 Selected Issues by Percent of Total Number of Selected Political Stories in Charlotte *Observer* for Selected Periods

Issues	Percent of Total Number of Stories by Periods[1]				
	Jan-May	June	Jul-Sept	Oct	Nov-Dec
Vietnam*	15.0%	16.5%	24.1%	21.3%	22.7%
Education	4.3	4.5	2.4	3.8	2.8
Race relations	11.4	13.4	9.1	14.1	16.6
Youth, drugs, morals*	3.0	3.3	2.4	2.7	4.3
Economy, cost of living*	6.4	6.9	6.1	3.8	6.6
School busing*	5.8	1.9	2.6	1.6	0.0
U.S.S.R./Red China*	8.8	4.1	2.0	4.3	1.9
Watergate/gov't corrup*	2.6	1.9	3.7	9.4	3.8
Crime, law and order	11.4	14.1	15.0	9.0	16.1
Environment, pollution*	4.5	6.2	3.5	4.7	1.4
Candidate personality	0.3	0.4	0.8	0.4	0.0
National defense	1.0	1.2	1.2	0.2	0.5
General internat. relations	3.8	4.7	1.8	2.2	3.8
General campaign events	11.7	11.3	13.2	12.3	7.1
General campaign analysis	10.1%	9.5%	12.0%	9.9%	12.3%
Total percent	100.1%**	99.9%**	99.9%**	99.7%**	99.9%**
Total number	625	665	506	445	211

[1]*This table includes all news stories, feature stories, editorials, and/or columns carried by the Observer on the topics studied.*

These issues constitute the "official agenda" discussed in the Appendix.

**Does not equal 100 percent because of rounding.*

backs which sometimes occurred if they filed a story very much different from a wire service version of the same event.

How come, these editors seemed to ask, your story differs from the wire story—can't you get it right?! Little wonder that once an event or continuing news story clearly establishes itself, it keeps public attention and continues to make news. Charlotte media clearly reflected this in the 1972 news coverage.

However, it is possible for an issue to erupt suddenly on occasion and, as surely, to drop quickly away. News about governmental corruption in general and the Watergate episode in particular arose from small coverage in early 1972 to nearly one story of every ten (of the political news studied) by October. To a regular reader of the *Observer* such an increase surely would have been noticeable.

At the same time, news about the environment and pollution dropped away during the final two months of the year. While most news subjects are consistently treated by the *Observer*, particular issues do rise and fall as dictated by the particular news values of any given moment. In other words, the media agenda does vary over time.

Not all news items furthermore had an equal chance of either being treated as news rather than feature or being put on page one, according to additional analysis which focused on the type of news presented and the page upon which it appeared. Vietnam news comprised between one-fifth and one-fourth of all news stories in 1972 and this topic was a staple of the *Observer's* front page. In fact, Vietnam news constituted a third of the *Observer* front page during the final three months of 1972. Even if you tried, it would have been difficult to ignore this topic, at least if you looked at the front page.

Crime, law, and order was another topic which made up a major portion of the news coverage, often on the front page. By contrast, news about education rarely made the front page unless it involved the dramatic topic of busing. It seems that journalists regularly treat some topics as news rather than feature and, as regularly, tend to think of these topics as page one material.

News about governmental corruption and Watergate filled 10.1 percent of the general news coverage but 16.2 percent of the front page news in October, just a month before the election. When it comes to the news agenda, not all news topics are created equal. Conflict has the edge.

The break-in of Democratic Party headquarters in the Watergate apartment complex in Washington, D.C., and the subsequent attempts to cover-up information relative to that break-in (events which we loosely refer to as the Watergate scandal) eventually helped topple Mr. Nixon from power. But it took time. Watergate, in particular was front page news before the election. In other words, coverage dropped suddenly after the election. But as reporters Bob Woodward and Carl Bernstein of the Washington *Post* were to demonstrate, and Richard Nixon was to learn, to drop in immediate news importance is not necessarily to be forgotten.[4]

Television Emphasis in
June and October

While the *Observer* demonstrated the news agenda is subject to sudden change on occasion, this phenomenon is more striking in television news (see Table 3–2). Television news, of course, is even more confined by time limitations than newspapers are by space. You can add additional pages but you cannot add more news time without preempting a predetermined program schedule. Television news therefore often skips from major topic to major topic, leaving newspapers and magazines to fill in the lesser topics and give depth to major stories.[5] *Shaw*

Vietnam news consistently took up about a fourth of the news coverage of the network evening broadcasts, about the same as in the *Observer* (see Table 3–2). But all three networks greatly increased coverage of news of the economy and the cost of living—campaign issues emphasized by Senator McGovern—by October, while *Observer* coverage of this news actually declined from 6.9 percent in June to 3.8 percent by October.

On Watergate, however, networks and *Observer* agreed. By October, the networks as well as *Observer* heavily played coverage of governmental corruption and Watergate. Clearly

Table 3-2 Selected Issues Emphasized by Networks and Charlotte Observer in June and October

Issues	Networks						Newspaper	
	ABC		CBS		NBC		Charlotte Observer	
	June	Oct	June	Oct	June	Oct	June	Oct
Vietnam*	22.1%	20.7%	27.0%	19.4%	23.4%	17.9%	16.5%	21.3%
Youth, drugs, morals*	1.0	2.1	0.0	1.6	1.4	1.7	3.3	2.7
Economy, cost of living*	4.0	14.5	4.4	15.9	3.7	12.1	6.9	3.8
School busing*	2.5	4.5	2.2	3.2	1.9	1.2	1.9	1.6
U.S.S.R./Red China*	3.0	0.3	2.6	1.9	5.1	3.5	4.1	4.3
Watergate/gov't corrup*	2.0	9.3	1.8	6.5	4.7	8.4	1.9	9.4
Environment/pollution*	4.5	0.7	4.0	1.0	2.8	2.6	6.2	4.7
General internatl. relations	15.1	1.4	13.7	2.6	9.3	4.6	4.7	2.2
General campaign events	25.1	11.0	22.1	7.4	34.1	10.4	11.3	12.4
General campaign analysis	2.0	7.6	1.0	5.8	0.5	2.9	9.5	9.9
Other	18.6%	28.0%	21.2%	34.6%	13.1%	34.7%	33.7%	27.6%
Total percent	99.9%**	100.1%**	100.0%	99.9%**	100.0%	100.0%	100.0%	99.9%**
Total number	199 .	290	226	309	214	346	665	445

*These issues constitute the "official agenda" discussed in the Appendix.
**Does not equal 100 percent because of rounding.

this was emerging as an important news area to the media whether all voters thought so or not.[6]

As interest in President Richard Nixon's trip to China died away and news interest focused on the upcoming presidential nominations and election itself, coverage of general international relations declined. Campaign analysis (mostly speculation about who was going to win, often based on political polls released by candidates) absorbed about a tenth of the coverage in the *Observer* in June and October. By October, campaign analysis had increased on all three networks.

The content analysis results reported in Tables 3–1 and 3–2 show that both the *Observer* and networks emphasized a relatively wide range of major issues. Some issues such as Vietnam and governmental corruption took a heavy share, but the economy, education, crime, and many other areas of community concern were covered on a regular basis if not always heavily emphasized. The emphasis placed on any given news event or topic can vary considerably over a short period of time, as was true in 1972 with the erupting Watergate issue and news of the economy.

Audience interests, candidate strategy, and media news values all play a part in determining what campaign news is carried. However, the final result of this mix of interests is an agenda of news topics—the building blocks of public issues—which cannot always be predicted.

Intermedia Agreement

Reflecting common reportorial values and focus on the same news events, news information overlaps a great deal from medium to medium. As was true in other studies,[7] this similarity emerged in Charlotte where there was relatively high agreement in news topic emphasis among the three networks studied and between the networks and the Charlotte *Observer* (see Table 3–3).

Table 3-3 Intra- and Intermedia Correlations of the 7 "Official Agenda" Issues for June and October

| | | June | | | |
		ABC	CBS	NBC	Charlotte Observer
	ABC		+.96	+.57	+.90
	CBS	+.89		+.61	+.94
October					
	NBC	+.64	+.75		+.45
	Charlotte Observer	+.64	+.64	+.93	

The agreement among media generally was higher in October than in June. This may reflect increased consensus on the "true" issues by journalists as the campaign comes to a conclusion. Voters watching any one of the networks and reading the Observer would be very likely to see the same news topics emphasized again and again. If voters tend to use the media more as the campaign comes to a conclusion—they did in this study—then the potential for an agenda-setting effect is increased. Not only is there greater media use, there is a greater likelihood of seeing the same topics.

Charlotte Voters and Their Issues of Importance

Voters, of course, intentionally and unintentionally learn information from a variety of sources. Most people probably are not even aware of where they learn about many public affairs events, especially as these events recede into the past. Only dramatic events such as the assassination of a President impress us so strongly that we remember, often for years, how we learned about the event. Nearly everyone who remembers the assassination of President John F. Kennedy in 1963 or civil rights leader Martin Luther King in 1968 remembers how he learned of these events. For most voters, however, impressions of public affairs and political leaders are built up from snatches of radio broadcasts heard on the way home from work or school, television newscasts blasting away through supper and noisy kids, and newspaper stories tucked here and there from front page through the sports pages.

Voters also learn from family, friends, and co-workers, with women more likely to be influenced by family and men influenced more by co-workers, as one might expect from typical work patterns.[8] The challenge of agenda-setting research is to determine how much issue patterns are built up directly from voter exposure to news media or indirectly from exposure to influential people whose ideas were influenced by the media. How much of the total does media political news contribute?

In Charlotte, voters reflected some clearly defined patterns in expressing issue concerns important to them. For young male voters, Vietnam constituted the most important issue in both June and October, but by October the economy and cost of living—bread and butter issues—were rising in importance for this group as well as for other voters. The young expressed themselves in other ways; they generally tended to be less concerned than older voters about drugs and morals while they expressed more concern about environmental pollution, particularly by October.

For older voters, the economy and cost of living were the leading issues in June and the margin of this lead had increased by October. Many of these voters were no doubt trapped between fixed incomes and inflation. Demographics, while crude indicators, can help locate the political issues which interest us.

Watergate and governmental crime concerned roughly one in five in June 1972, the month the Watergate break-in story first broke open, but interest actually declined for Charlotte voters as a whole by October. For many voters Watergate may have been a partisan, red herring issue.[9] Of those concerned, women more often than men and those of middle age (31–55) more often than younger or older voters cited a concern about governmental corruption.

The Study's
Official Agenda

The seven issues selected for in-depth study as an "official" agenda held up reasonably well during the June and October periods. These issues represented three types.

First, the primarily true public issues were Watergate and governmental corruption and the Nixon visit to Red China. These are areas which do not personally affect voters. To know or care about them, voters would have to learn about them directly or indirectly from news media. The media devoted major news emphasis to the Nixon visit to Red China early in 1972, including much editorial and columnist discussion of the relationship between the two nations. Likewise, major news attention was devoted to the stories about the break-in of the Democratic Party headquarters. Charlotte voters as a group clearly responded to both news areas, reflecting more interest in both during June when the Nixon trip was more recent and the Watergate story was hotter news.

Second, three issues selected for the official agenda fell into both public and private concern, depending on the particular situation of the individual voter. Vietnam news was one example and this issue proved important to most voters but particularly to the young males who were, of course, most vulnerable to actual call-up for war. Busing news indexed an area of concern to voters of the 31 to 55 age range. These voters often had children whom this directly affected. For many other voters the busing issue appears to have been more academic. Finally news about youth, drugs, and morals found a more ready audience among older voters for whom the issue may not always have been academic because of their children than

among younger voters who may have obtained their information on the streets. Such issues can be public or private; it depends upon the angle from which you are viewing the news.

Third, two issues included in the study official agenda represented more private than public concerns. One, the economy
and cost of living, affects all voters. In Charlotte, older voters
showed much more responsiveness to this than did younger
voters. They no doubt had more at stake. The reverse generally
was true about the environment and pollution, an issue in
which younger voters appeared more interested and sensitive.

These issues were selected for correlational analysis
throughout the Charlotte study to represent a range of issues
indexed by the news. The range includes issues, as we have
seen, which were mostly public, mostly private or those which
could be either, depending upon the background and problems
of the individual voter. All issues cited by voters or news areas
covered by the news media were not included because evidence suggests that voters do not keep in mind more than about
five to seven significant issues at any given time.[10] Put another
way, there is a general consensus among voters in the aggregate regarding a few, select issues. These issues can change
throughout the campaign. Here, for example, we saw an increase in the importance of the economic issue at the end of the
campaign. This may have reflected major television news emphasis as well as continued worsening of the economic situation as 1972 progressed.

On the other hand, voters may not increase their interest in
any given issue merely because the media have increased emphasis. A major step-up in coverage of Watergate-related
events did not result in an immediate increase in Charlotte
voter interest in the issue of government corruption. It may be
that for public issues like Watergate, media effects result only
from emphasis over a long period of time or when the issue
achieves major front page and television coverage.[11] After all,
even the crude label Watergate masks a whole series of complex and interrelated events touching on governmental
honesty, presidential performance, and the administration of

justice. In short, a Watergate, whatever that means to individual voters, does not press nearly so hard against voter consciousness as an empty pocketbook.

For the researcher who has to establish well beforehand what media issues he will content analyze and what issues to ask voters about, the study challenge is to select issues which span a variety of public concerns and which will last throughout the campaign. In this study, the seven issues selected appear to have held up reasonably well. Even though the public issues are probably the least important to voters, yet they have proven to be issues upon which the news media studied supplied important voter information.

Media Use During the Campaign

As the day of election approaches, those planning to vote need to make a final decision about who they will support. For those who are deeply partisan, of course, that choice long since has been made—merely being labeled Republican or Democratic is cue enough.[12] Increasingly, however, scholars are finding that many American voters carefully sort out *issues*, do *not* merely respond to personalities or party labels, and split their votes between the parties in support of candidates who have taken a stand on issues which they like.[13] For these voters, political information may be important right up to the day of election, particularly information related to new developments on issues.

At any rate, Charlotte voters made greater use of news media as the campaign came to an end. This was particularly true of television (see Table 3-4). Those using television "a great deal" increased by October, although those using the *Observer* "a great deal" slightly declined in number. But including voters who said they used the *Observer* "some," usage of the *Observer* also increased by October. Fewer voters said they made little or no use of either media. This increased read-

Table 3–4 Television and Newspaper Use by Voters for June and
          October

Use	Television		Newspaper	
	June	October	June	October
A great deal	41.6%	51.1%	57.7%	54.0%
Some	36.3	35.1	26.4	34.1
Very little	19.5	8.9	13.2	9.3
None	2.6	4.9	2.6	2.6
Total percent	100.0%	100.0%	99.9%*	100.0%
Total Voters	226**	225**	227	226**

Does not equal 100 percent because of rounding.
**Does not equal 227 because of occasional voter nonresponse.*

ing and viewing in October could reflect some seasonal patterns as schools, which were closed in June, began and people
turned away from heavy outdoor summer activities. People
came back into the house and switched on the television set.

But it is as likely that voters increased news media reading
and viewing as the campaign came to a close and voters real-
ized they soon would have to make hard political choices. That
requires information. Whatever the reason, voters exposed
themselves to the media more often and thus increased the potential for agenda-setting effects. October is also the month
when candidates pour on their heaviest advertising so that
voters are likely to be exposed to more political information
from that source as well as from the news. The combination of
the actual oncoming election event and increased potential for
media news and advertising exposure makes the final days of
the campaign a time of great potential influence among those
still making up their minds.

Voters do not attend to the media alike, just as they differ
about public issues regarded as important. In June and October, women voters reported, more often than did men, using
television news "a great deal"; women's usage of newspapers

was slightly greater in June but much more in October. Taking into account voters who claimed to read the Observer either a "great deal" or "some," men voters more than women voters read the Observer in both June and October. Fewer men than women said they read the Observer "very little" or "none." But men voters slightly more than women voters said they saw little or no television news. Men voters seemed a bit more print oriented; women voters were slightly more television oriented when it came to political news.

Voters of all ages viewed television news more heavily in October than in June. For the Observer, voters claiming to read the paper "a great deal" declined somewhat except for the 31 to 55 age group. If you take voters claiming to read/view "some" or "a great deal" together, young voters (30 or less) made greater use of television news and less of the Observer as the campaign ended while voters older than 30 made more use of the Observer and about the same use of television news. Perhaps television has been a more integral part of the lives of those 30 or younger while older voters, having been raised on newspapers, use them more loyally.[14]

Voters and Television:
The Agenda-Setting Phenomenon

Wilbur Schramm, long one of the nation's leading mass communication scholars, has argued that the effects of mass media are gradual, similar to the way rock formations are built up in a cave by slowly dripping calcareous water.[15]

On the other hand, on rare occasions the mass media can have powerful and immediate audience effects. The 1938 radio program "Invasion from Mars" was such an example. This play about an invasion of earth sent hundreds of people into the streets to "escape" and seriously disturbed thousands who did not take to the streets.[16] Likewise the widespread public reaction, that led to rioting in some cases, following the 1968 assassination of Martin Luther King was attributable to some degree to mass media coverage.[17] For researchers focusing on agenda-setting, the question is: *If there are agenda-setting effects on voters resulting from exposure to mass media, are these effects "short-range," "long-range," or in the case of different issues, both?*

In the Charlotte study there is evidence of a limited short-range effect (see Table 3–5). Comparing what voters cited as important to them[18] with what the major television networks said shows that the agenda-setting effect is stronger for October, a time of heavier viewing, than was true in June for CBS and NBC viewers. Voters who claim to watch a medium more

Table 3–5 Heavy vs. Light Media Users: How Well Do They Agree with the Media Issues Emphasized?[1]

Television Use	June		October		Amount Change (October minus June)[2]	
	CBS	NBC	CBS	NBC	CBS	NBC
Some—Great deal	+.33	+.21	+.68	+.64	+.35	+.43
Little—None	+.41	+.05	+.60	+.20	+.19	+.15
Difference[2]	−.08	+.16	+.08	+.44	+.16	+.28
Observer Use						
Some—Great deal	+.39		+.28		−.11	
Little—None	+.63		+.23		−.40	
Difference	−.24		+.05		+.29	

[1]The "official agenda" issues mentioned by voters who claimed to use television some or a great deal are compared with the emphasis placed on these issues by the network cited as most watched. Few Charlotte voters said they regularly watched ABC network news so ABC is not included in this analysis.

[2]These differences are measured in the direction predicted by the agenda-setting hypothesis, namely that those with greater exposure to a medium will be more influenced by that medium and that news media are more influential as the campaign concludes and voters arrive at their final voting choices.

heavily theoretically should be more influenced by that medium, While the differences are not strong, voters who said they watched television more, better reflected the network issue emphasis than did voters who said they watched less. The exception was CBS light viewers in June who were closer in agreement than were heavier viewers. For NBC and its viewers in October the case was stronger; in all, three of four correlations went in the predicted direction.

The extent of agreement with the network news coverage increased relatively more for voters watching television more often than for those using television less often (see Table 3–5). This argues that not only does television have greater potential influence to shape voter perception of issues at the end of a campaign, but that this potential is greater for voters claiming to make more use of television. These voters, of course, were more often exposed to the television issue stimulus. These comparisons of the television news agenda with voters' issue agendas at two points in time provide some evidence of an important relationship between what the television screen is saying and voters are thinking about.

The case for *Observer* readers by contrast cannot be made for a short-range agenda-setting effect. Those who made little or no use of the *Observer* in June were more in agreement with the way the *Observer* emphasized agenda issues than were those reading more heavily. This pattern was reversed, but very weakly, for the *Observer* and readers in October. There was no short-range agenda-setting effect for the *Observer*. Voters reading the *Observer* in October did tend to agree somewhat more with the *Observer* issue emphasis if they read the paper more often but there is not much evidence of agenda-setting.

Short-range tests are the most difficult to use when determining agenda-setting effects because they implicitly argue that mass media are very powerful immediate influencers of our cognitions. Humans, however, are (fortunately) resistant to instant adoption of and belief in every idea which comes along. One might assert with Schramm, better tests of mass media agenda-setting would result from looking at mass media effects over a longer period of time.[19] There is some evidence, as we shall see, that media agenda-setting in fact is a long-range process, involving a time lag of several weeks or even months. Like Rome, press influence cannot be built in a day.

NOTES

[1]An interesting study of professional norms is Jack M. McLeod and Searle E. Hawley, Jr., "Professionalism Among Newsmen," *Journalism Quarterly*, 41:529–38 (Autumn 1964).

[2]Many studies demonstrating the heavy use made of wire services are cited in Donald L. Shaw, "Surveillance vs. Constraint: Press Coverage of a Social Issue," *Journalism Quarterly*, 46:707–12 (Winter 1969).

[3]See Timothy Crouse, *The Boys On The Bus* (New York: Ballantine Books, 1972), p. 10.

[4]Carl Bernstein and Bob Woodward, *All the President's Men* (New York: Warner Paperback, 1975).

[5]See Donald L. Shaw, "The 1971 Economic Freeze: From Event to Issue," in Maxwell McCombs (ed.), "Working Papers on Agenda-Setting," University of North Carolina School of Journalism, July 1973.

[6]See David Weaver, Maxwell E. McCombs, and Charles Spellman, "Watergate and the Media: A Case Study of Agenda-Setting," *American Politics Quarterly*, 3:458–72 (October 1975).

[7]See McCombs and Shaw, *op. cit.*

[8]The importance of interpersonal communications for voters became clear in an early, "classic" study: Paul Lazarsfeld, Bernard Berelson, and Hazel Gaudet, *The People's Choice* (New York: Columbia University Press, 1948). The importance of interpersonal communications in areas other than politics was well established in Elihu Katz and Paul F. Lazarsfeld, *Personal Influence* (New York: The Free Press, 1955).

[9]Mr. Nixon seemed to imply in some public statements that publicity related to the incidents associated with the break-in of the Watergate apartment complex in Washington was politically motivated to embarass him.

[10]A study which focuses on the number of agenda issues regarded as important by a special group is William Thomas Gormley, Jr., "Newspaper Agendas and Political Elites," *Journalism Quarterly*, 52:304–08. (Summer 1975).

[11]The possibility of a time "lag" between time of media mention and time of voter cognitive "response" is discussed in Donald L. Shaw and Cynthia L. Long, "Voters and Issues: A Study of Media Agenda-Setting in the 1972 Campaign," Report prepared for the National Association of Broadcasters, University of North Carolina School of Journalism, January 1975.

[12]The influence of political party affiliation, while perhaps less strong today than it was 20 years ago, has been documented in many important early studies. See Lazarsfeld *et. al., op. cit.,* and Bernard Berelson, Paul Lazarsfeld, and W. McPhee, *Voting* (Chicago: University of Chicago Press, 1954).

[13]See Walter DeVries and V. Lance Tarrance, Jr., *The Ticker-Splitter: A New Force in American Politics* (Grand Rapids: William B. Eerdmans Publishing Company, 1972). Also see David M. Kovenock, James W. Prothro, and Associates, *Explaining the Vote. Part II, Presidential Choices in Individual States* (Chapel Hill: Institute for Research in Social Science, 1973). Both are among some recent studies which find increased importance for issues in political choices.

[14]Older and better educated readers appear among newspapers' most loyal supporters. See Bruce H. Westley and Werner J. Severin, "A Profile of the Daily Newspaper Non-Reader," *Journalism Quarterly*, 41:45–50 and 156 (Winter 1964); and Jeanne Penrose, David H. Weaver, Richard R. Cole, and Donald L. Shaw, "The Newspaper Nonreader 10 Years Later: A Partial Replication of Westley-Severin," *Journalism Quarterly*, 51:631–38 (Winter 1974).

[15]Wilbur Schramm, "The Effects of Mass Communications: A Review," *Journalism Quarterly*, 26:397–409 (December 1949).

[16]See Hadley Cantril, *The Invasion From Mars* (New York: Harper, 1966). Originally published by Princeton University in 1940.

[17]For an interesting reflection on the relationship between media coverage and social disruptions see "The News Media and the Disorders," in *Report of the National Advisory Commission on Civil Disorders* (New York: Bantam Books, Inc., 1968), pp. 362–389.

[18]See appendix for exact wordings of all questions.

[19]Schramm, *op. cit.*

*

4 Candidate Advertising: The Agenda is the Message

THOMAS A. BOWERS
University of North Carolina at Chapel Hill

The real question in political advertising is how to surround the voter with the proper auditory and visual stimuli to evoke the reaction you want for him, i.e., his voting for a specific candidate.

Tony Schwartz, *The Responsive Chord*

News is only part of each campaign's flood of political communication. Another major element is political advertising, especially on television. Televised political advertising has become the perennial whipping post of modern political campaigns. Critics charge that it costs too much and gives an advantage to the well-heeled candidate, that it demeans the electoral process by emphasizing what a candidate looks like instead of what he says, or that it is downright dishonest. There are very few supporters of televised political advertising—except perhaps the consultants and the media which benefit financially. Few candidates feel safe in supporting it, but few feel safe in ignoring it. Candidates apparently feel it would be political suicide to vocally support something so universally disliked, yet political suicide to wage a campaign without it.

In recent years, social scientists have begun to pay closer attention to televised political advertising, primarily to ascertain what effect, if any, it has upon the voters. The Charlotte study provided an opportunity to analyze televised political advertising from the agenda-setting perspective.

During a political campaign, candidates play active roles in the agenda-setting process. They try to convey their agendas to voters through the mass media. Before elections, candidates ascertain the relative importance of problems voters perceive. While some candidates rely upon intuition, many spend large amounts of money for sophisticated and expensive public opinion polls to learn how voters feel about issues. Relying primarily upon this advance information, candidates set their agendas—the issues they will emphasize during the campaign.

Because it is impossible to deliver a message personally to all voters, the candidate necessarily must rely upon the media. But will the media emphasize issues the way he or she wants? You can never be sure.

The candidate can exercise direct control through his advertising, however, and can exercise indirect influence by making speeches and policy statements on selected issues—behavior he hopes will be reported by news media. His objective, of course, is to convince voters he is better qualified than his opponent to handle the very problems voters consider important.[1]

The candidate evaluates the effectiveness of his agenda-setting on election day: if he wins, he probably considers it effective; if he loses, he most likely considers it ineffective. From a research perspective, however, we were interested in more than whether a particular candidate won. We were interested in how well the *candidate* agenda was conveyed by media news and advertising and how well voters learned that agenda.

Candidates and the
Advertising Agenda

One major question, of course, is how closely candidates' agendas correspond to voters' agendas. Without access to inside strategy statements, we necessarily inferred candidate agendas from issues emphasized in their television advertising. The candidates control their advertising far more than the news written about them.

The content of the advertising was determined by monitoring the three television networks during prime time on weeknights for the nearly three weeks voters were interviewed in the October wave. All Nixon and McGovern commercials, regardless of length, were coded for the frequency with which certain issues were mentioned. These frequencies were summed to give the candidates' agendas of issues in their advertising.[2]

The agendas of the Charlotte voters, the presidential candidates, and the news media reported in this chapter do not correspond exactly to the "official" or standard agendas reported elsewhere in this book (see Table 4–1). The basis for the agendas in this chapter was the list of issues cited by the candidates in their television advertising, not just the issues mentioned in the news. Added to that was the issue of education, mentioned by voters but ignored by both candidates in the advertising we monitored. It was necessary to combine a few categories to make the agendas of issues in the newspaper and network television news correspond to the voter agendas found in the survey and candidates' agendas represented in the ads.

For voters, the important issues were the economy, Vietnam, drugs, welfare and education, and governmental corruption. In the Nixon ads, the most frequently mentioned issues were candidate personality, Vietnam, foreign relations (primarily with China and the Soviet Union), welfare, the environment, and the economy. Not surprisingly perhaps, governmental corruption was not mentioned. The most frequently mentioned issues in McGovern ads were candidate personality, the

Table 4-1 A Comparison of the Agendas'[1] of Voters, Candidates, and Media in October

Voters	Nixon Ads	McGovern Ads	Newspaper News	National TV News
1. Economy	1. Personality	1. Personality	1. Vietnam	1. Vietnam
2. Vietnam	2. Vietnam	2. Economy	2. Busing	2. Economy
3. Drugs	3. Foreign Relations	3. Vietnam	3. Corruption	3. Corruption
4. Welfare	4. Welfare	4. Welfare	4. Crime	4. Foreign Relations
5. Education	5. Environment	5. Corruption	5. Foreign Relations	5. Busing
6. Corruption	6. Economy	6. Environment	6. Environment	6. Drugs
7. Crime	7. Drugs	6. Defense	7. Economy	7. Environment
8. Busing	7. Busing	6. Busing	7. Education	8. Crime*
9. Environment	7. Defense	9. Foreign Relations	9. Drugs	8. Education*
10. Foreign Relations	10. 18-yr.-vote	9. Drugs	10. Personality	8. Personality*
11. Defense	11. Crime	9. Crime	11. Defense	8. Defense*
12. 18-yr.-vote*	12. Education*	12. 18-yr.-vote*	12. Welfare*	8. Welfare*
13. Personality*	13. Corruption*	13. Education*	12. 18-yr.-vote*	8. 18-yr.-vote*

*Means no mentions for this category.

[1] The issues cited in this table are not the "official" list of voter, Observer, or [combined] television news issues used elsewhere in this book. such as Chapter 3. The basis for this particular list was the issues cited by candidates in their television advertising and all other categories were made to conform as closely as possible for comparison. Added to this television advertising basic list, for example, was the issue of education. mentioned by some voters but ignored by both candidates in their advertising. It was necessary to combine a few categories to make the agenda of issues in the newspaper and the network television news correspond to the voter and candidates' agendas. The data on voters, including their agenda in Table 1. and other data in later tables. were collected during the October interviewing period.

economy, Vietnam, welfare, governmental corruption, and the environment.

The rank-order correlations between the voter agenda and the candidates' agendas were low: +.11 for the Nixon agenda and +.37 for the McGovern agenda (see Table 4–2). These low correlations can probably be explained in a number of ways. First, candidate polling to ascertain voter concerns, if done at all, is usually done very early in the campaign. Candidates might set their agendas then and stick by them while voter concerns could change by the end of the campaign.

Table 4–2 Spearman's Rank-order Correlations among the Agendas

	Voters	Nixon Ads	McGovern Ads	Newspaper	TV News
Voters	—	.11	.37	(See Chapter 3)	
Nixon ads	.38*	—	.65^a	-.05	.22
McGovern ads	.63*^{b}		—	.06	.26

*"Personality" item deleted from agendas
^{a}p < .01
^{b}p < .05

Second, even if candidates do have up-to-the-minute readings of voter concerns, their selection of issues can still be influenced by factors other than voter polls. In other words, candidates can avoid certain voter concerns (like Nixon avoiding the Watergate-corruption issue), or else they consider some issues more important than the voters do (like Nixon's emphasis upon relations with Russia and Red China). After all, candidates use ads to exert *their* issue interests.

The third explanation is methodological. Because voters were asked to name the problem or issue they were most concerned about, they did not name candidate personality, although this doubtless is important to many voters. Candidate advertising, on the other hand, included many references to such personality traits as honesty and credibility. Clearly, candidates treat personality—as filtered through television advertising—as an issue. If the personality item is removed from the candidates' and the voters' agendas, the correlations rise to +.38 for Nixon and +.63 for McGovern.

It is also apparent that many voters consider candidate personality a relevant issue. In fact, when we asked our Charlotte voters to tell how they would describe the presidential candidates to a friend, several used traits such as "firmness," presidential "stature" and "honesty." This tended to be true more for "heavy" than for "light" television viewers, suggesting the importance of television in conveying personality information. Apparently personality can reach through the television screen. In addition, the corruption issue cited as an important problem by several voters essentially revolved around the question of personal honesty. It would seem that some voters judge a candidate as much by how he acts as by what he says. Candidate personality, then, clearly can be an issue in political campaigns.

Candidate Versus
Media Agendas

Another question is: How well were the candidates' agendas transmitted into the media news agenda? We compared the issue emphasis in the candidates' advertising with the issue emphasis in the media news content—the closer the correspondence, the more successful the candidates were in getting their agendas transmitted.

If President Nixon and Senator McGovern did try to transmit the same agendas emphasized in their ads to voters through the news stories, they were not very successful. There was no correlation between the agenda of issues reported in the Charlotte *Observer* news and the two presidential candidates, and the correlations between the candidates' advertising agendas and the television news agenda were low (see Tables 4–1 and 4–2).

This lack of correspondence shows the difficulty candidates have in trying to get their agendas transmitted via the media news. Perhaps it shows that reporters have strong minds of their own. At any rate, candidates are often forced to deviate from their planned agenda of issues during the campaign. George McGovern, for example, made several speeches on Vietnam late in the campaign because his staff believed it would bring in more contributions from supporters already committed to him and not because the staff or McGovern felt it was a particularly important issue for all voters.[3]

News media, of course, act independently and sometimes defiantly refuse to follow a candidate's agenda. Many reporters covering New York Mayor John Lindsay in the 1972 primaries, for instance, apparently were so concerned with exposing him as what some felt to be a media-image candidate that they did not report what he was saying about issues.[4] One of the very reasons candidates use advertising is because they have more control over the content and are sometimes able to counter or correct unfavorable treatment they may receive in the news.

Who Saw the Advertising?

Another question is whether voters even saw the television advertising, because they could not learn anything from the commercials unless they were exposed to them. Exposure to advertising is difficult to measure. Because it was impractical directly to observe voters' exposure to advertising, we had to rely upon their memory and ask them how much advertising they could recall seeing for each of the two candidates.

It is logical that persons who watch television a great deal would see and recall more political advertising than voters who watched less television. Atkin et al found such a relationship and reported that voters really could not avoid political advertising on television.[5] We hypothesized therefore that high use of television for political news would be positively related to high recall of televised political advertising and low use to low recall.

Voters who reported high use of television were significantly more likely to recall seeing commercials for the candidates than were voters who reported low use of television (see Tables 4–3 and 4–4). The hypothesis was supported: exposure to television is related to exposure to commercials and is probably due a great deal to incidental exposure. Few, if any, voters actually seek to view television commercials.

About one-third of the voters reported they could not recall seeing any advertising for either candidate. Even if these voters did see some political advertising, it apparently did not make a lasting impression. However, the interviews were conducted in October and candidates typically step up their advertising program during the very last days of the campaign. It might have been that this late volume of advertising overcame even these voters' inattention, although we did not study them later.

What kinds of voters did recall seeing political advertising? White voters were more likely to recall seeing "many" commercials for both Nixon and McGovern than were black voters. These data are not shown in tables, but in the case of McGovern ads at least, exposure to or recall of the advertising was also related to income: as income increased, so did the proportion of voters who could recall seeing "many" of his commercials. There was evidence of a similar, but weaker relationship in the case of Nixon advertising. Surlin and Gordon also have reported greater recall of political advertising for voters higher in socioeconomic status.[6] Unfortunately there were too few McGovern supporters in the panel of voters to permit analysis of possible selective exposure to or recall of advertising.[7]

Table 4–3 Relationship between Use of Television for Political News and Recall of Nixon Commercials

Use of Television
for Political News   *Recall of Nixon Commercials*

	None	Few	Many	Total	Number
Not at all	45.5%	54.5%	—	100%	(11)
Very little	60.9	34.8	1.0	100	(23)
Some	30.5	57.3	12.2	100	(82)
Great deal	26.6	45.2	28.2	100	(124)

Chi Square = 22.47, df = 6, p < .01

Table 4–4 Relationship between Use of Television for Political News and Recall of McGovern Commercials

Use of Television
for Political News   *Recall of McGovern Commercials*

	None	Few	Many	Total	Number
Not at all	72.7%	27.3%	–	100%	(11)
Very little	59.1	40.9	–	100	(22)
Some	28.9	59.0	12.0	100	(83)
Great deal	28.7	51.6	19.7	100	(122)

Chi Square = 20.76, df = 6, p<.01

What Did Voters Learn from Advertising?

Our ultimate interest is the cognitive effects resulting from advertising—what voters actually learn from what they see. One thing voters could have learned was the agendas of issues which President Nixon and Senator McGovern emphasized in their television commercials.

The correspondence between the agenda of issues recalled from the advertising and the actual advertising agenda would be one measure of voter learning. Because repetition of themes in ads gradually builds up the salience of certain issues associated with a candidate, we hypothesized that high exposure to a candidate's advertising would be related positively to accuracy in recalling the issue salience of that advertising. The agenda of voters who could recall seeing "many" commercials for a candidate would more closely match the candidate's advertising agenda than would the agenda of voters who could recall seeing only "a few" commercials. In short, did exposed voters learn from the ads?

The hypothesized relationship did not hold in the case of Nixon advertising. The rank-order correlation was +.38 for voters recalling "many" but +.60 for those voters recalling "a few." The hypothesis was supported in the case of McGovern advertising, however. The correlation was +.20 for voters recalling "many" commercials and −.42 for those recalling "a few." In other words, there is some evidence that voters did learn the McGovern agenda in his televised advertising. Patterson and McClure also concluded that televised advertising was effective in communicating information relating to the beliefs that voters held about the candidates.[8]

Advertising and "Affect"

It is likely that voters learn more than just the agenda of issues stressed by the candidates. They probably absorb affect or feeling as well as issue information. In other words voters acquire affect about candidates—"he is an honest man"—along with the more issue-oriented advertising. This would seem to be more true for voters who were exposed to a great deal of television advertising. By combining sight, sound, and motion, television is better able to convey emotional feelings or to evoke those feelings in viewers than can print media.

This affect, too, may be negative as well as positive. In other words, in their normal, day-to-day exposure to the mass media—and particularly television—during the political campaign, voters learn information about both candidates and they learn information both favorable and unfavorable to each candidate. McCombs and Shaw found, for example, that voter concerns (their political agenda) were more closely correlated with all the news in the media than with the news just about their own party.[9]

We hypothesized therefore that high exposure to television advertising is positively related to high affect (positive or negative) in describing a candidate, while low exposure is related to low affect. Out of sight *may* be out of mind.

Salience of affect was operationalized as the obvious presence of emotion or feeling in the voter's role-playing description of each candidate. The voter was asked: "Suppose there was someone who was undecided about whom to vote for in the presidential election. What would you tell that person about each candidate?" There was no probing and respondents could answer strictly in terms of issues, personality, or both issues and personality. The responses which were more dominant in feeling or emotion—over more rational listing or discussion of issues—were judged "high affect;" those with the reverse pattern were judged "low affect."

Some examples of "high affect" responses are: "He's too far out." "He's two-faced." "He's awfully wishy-washy." "He's shifty and can't be trusted." "He will end this senseless war right away." Some examples of low affect responses are: "He has strengthened relations with communist countries." "He's afraid of domestic problems." "He has a sincere concern for the poor." "Some of his economic ideas have not been good." "I feel he is an honest man." After two training sessions, intercoder reliability among three coders was .80, which was deemed acceptable. Coders can break down these answers into two groups reasonably well but judgments finer than two are difficult to make.

The hypothesis that voters would absorb affect along with issue information failed in the case of Nixon. His commercials apparently did not generate much affect among voters. In fact, voters who could recall few or no Nixon commercials expressed greater affect than voters who had seen many commercials (see Table 4–5). To some extent this may have resulted because voters had long seen Nixon on television. His commercials—and there were many in which he did not appear—may have reinforced older views rather than raised new affective saliences. Additional analysis suggests, too, that voters held much stronger feelings about McGovern (both positive and negative) than about Nixon, toward whom many voters apparently felt neutral.[10]

For the McGovern commercials, the hypothesis was supported—high exposure to McGovern televised advertising ap-

Table 4–5 Relationship between Recall of Commercials and Salience of Affect

Recall of Nixon Commercials	Salience of Affect			
	Low	High	Total	Number
None	63.8%	36.2%	100%	(72)
Few	63.1	36.9	100	(103)
Many	82.2	17.8	100	(45)

Chi Square = 5.76, (ns)

Recall of McGovern Commercials				
None	66.7%	33.3%	100%	(72)
Few	46.8	53.2	100	(111)
Many	45.7	54.3	100	(35)

Chi Square = 7.83, df = 2, p<.05

parently led to higher affect (both positive and negative) in describing him (see Table 4-5). If we make a side-by-side comparison of the "high affect" percentages for Nixon and McGovern (Table 4-6), it is apparent that the McGovern advertising generated more affect among the more heavily-exposed than did the Nixon advertising. Significantly, much of that affect was very negative.

Table 4-6 Relationship between Recall of Commercials and High Salience of Affect in describing each candidate

Recall of Commercials	"High affect" in description of	
	Nixon	McGovern
None	36%	33%
Few	37	53
Many	18	54

McGovern's was a new face at the presidential level and he was not well known. Hence, voters had a greater need for orientation about him—more room to learn new information and feelings. McCombs has cited orientational need in explaining why newspaper editorials were more influential when talking about relatively minor issues, about which voters knew little, than about major issues or candidates about which or whom people already had well-developed feelings or information.[11]

Voters had much to learn about McGovern; what they learned, apparently with the aid of television advertising, did not prove entirely pleasing to Senator McGovern or the Democratic cause. Much has been written elsewhere about the problems of the McGovern campaign—the wavering and eventual elimination of support for Missouri Senator Thomas Eagleton as vice presidential nominee or the $1,000 per person welfare payments. It may be true that Senator McGovern closely matched the voter agenda with his advertising emphasis on the economy, Vietnam, welfare, and corruption. Ironically, however, he may have unknowingly been building the salience of issues most damaging to his cause.

In other words, it is likely that each time a McGovern commercial about welfare appeared, it aroused or reinforced negative feelings in voters critical of his proposals. The commercials might have benefited him if they had been seen only by his supporters. But that cannot be; incidental learning from exposure to televised advertising applies to critics as well as supporters.

NOTES

[1] For a more detailed description of candidate agenda-setting behavior and its concomitant problems see Thomas A. Bowers, "Political Advertising: Setting the Candidate's Agenda," Paper presented to National Conference on the Agenda-Setting Function of the Press, Syracuse University, October 1974.

[2] Inter-coder reliability was .88.

[3] Ernest R. May and Janet Fraser (eds.), *Campaign '72: The Managers Speak* (Cambridge: Harvard University Press, 1973), p. 27.

[4] James M. Perry, *Us & Them: How the Press Covered the 1972 Election* (New York: Clarkson N. Potter, 1973), pp. 52–59.

[5] Charles K. Atkin, Lawrence Bowen, Oguz B. Nayman, and Kenneth C. Sheinkopf, "Quality versus Quantity in Televised Political Ads," *Public Opinion Quarterly*, 37:209–24 (Summer 1973).

[6] Stuart H. Surlin and Thomas F. Gordon, "Selective Exposure and Retention of Political Advertising: A Regional Comparison," Paper presented to International Communication Association, New Orleans, 1974.

[7] There were insufficient cases to control for exposure—which would have allowed us to see if exposure was a function of race and income. There was no relationship between recall of commercials and sex, age and education level.

[8]See Thomas E. Patterson and Robert D. McClure, *Political Advertising: Voter Reaction to Televised Political Commercials* (Princeton: Citizens' Research Foundation, 1974).

[9]Maxwell E. McCombs and Donald L. Shaw, "The Agenda-Setting Function of Mass Media," *Public Opinion Quarterly,* 36:176–87 (Summer 1972).

[10]See *Newsweek,* November 13, 1972, pp. 30–31; and *Time,* November 6, 1972, pp. 42–43.

[11]Maxwell E. McCombs, "Editorial Endorsements: A Study of Influence," *Journalism Quarterly,* 44:545–48 (Autumn 1967).

*

5 The Interpersonal Agenda

EUGENE F. SHAW
University of Tennessee

An unconditional right to say what one pleases about public affairs is what I consider to be the minimum guarantee of the First Amendment.

Justice Hugo Black in N.Y. *Times Co.* v. *Sullivan*

An election campaign invariably ranks high on our agenda of what to talk about. This in itself may be an instance of the agenda-setting power of the press. The campaign provides the press with much of its copy—particularly for the front page of the daily newspaper and, as the campaign progresses, for the lead items on national news broadcasts. It is the story of the season, no matter which election year.

Alternatively, the electorate's interest in the campaign may be neither generated nor fostered primarily by the press but by other situational and behavioral factors: a candidate's campaigning in the area, stepped-up local activity of political parties, or even exposure to political talk at work, home, or social gatherings. Cocktail talk may not always be chatter. It is on such occasions that national problems often are discussed as campaign issues, a transmutation encouraged by political organizations, candidates, and press commentators.

Talking During a Campaign

Whatever the reason, people talk a lot about national issues and politics, especially as a campaign nears its end. In the 1972 presidential campaign, more than 40 percent of Charlotte voters were discussing politics at least once or twice a week as early as June. By October more than 60 percent of Charlotte voters reported participation in weekly political discussions.

When Charlotte voters did discuss politics, more than 10 percent admitted they "have definite ideas and try to convince" others to their viewpoint. And almost a third of the voters claimed they "take an equal share in (such) conversations," expressing their own opinions on political matters as well as listening to the views of others. Who these others were with whom Charlotte voters most frequently discussed politics apparently remained relatively fixed through the summer months and into the early fall. For most voters, the most frequent discussion partner was a member of the immediate family.

Differences in
Political Talk by Sex

This favoring of intra-family discussions was due primarily to the sex difference among the sample voters. In contrast with women, men voters discussed politics most often with people other than family or personal friends. The family provided most of the discussants for the Charlotte women voters and this trend increased as the campaign came toward an end. Women, of course, generally are home more than men.

Of all the demographic factors, sex was the best predictor of partner preference for a political discussion among Charlotte voters (see Table 5–1). Republicans and younger voters (those under 35 years old) showed the greatest diversity at each reading and the highest constancy over time in choice of those with whom they wanted to talk politics.

Among the more interesting contrasts, by income and education, is the difference between the lowest and highest categories in the proportion of "no responses"—those who either refused to name a discussion partner or could not do so because they never discuss politics. By October these high proportions of "no responses" in the lowest categories of the two

Table 5–1 Discussion Partners for Political Conversations, by Sex, Age, Income, Education, and Party Preference

	In June			
	Family	Friends	Others	No Response
Total Sample (N=227)	44%	25%	24%	7%
Male (N=86)	31	19	45	5
Female (N=141)	51	29	11	9
Under 35 years (N=62)	37	27	32	3
35–44 years (N=50)	52	20	24	4
45–54 years (N=57)	49	21	26	4
55 years or more (N=58)	38	31	14	17
Under $5,000 (N=22)	32	36	14	18
$5,000–$10,000 (N=66)	36	27	26	11
More than $10,000 (N=123)	49	22	29	2
Not a high-school graduate (N=31)	23	26	26	26
High-school graduate (N=56)	50	30	13	7
Some college education (N=82)	45	24	27	4
College graduate (N=58)	47	21	31	2
Democrat (N=154)	46	26	21	7
Republican (N=65)	40	23	31	6

Table 5-1 (cont'd)

	In October			
	Family	Friends	Others	No Response
Total Sample (N=227)	52%	24%	21%	3%
Male (N=86)	34	27	38	1
Female (N=141)	63	23	10	4
Under 35 years (N=62)	40	26	34	0
35–44 years (N=50)	56	22	20	2
45–54 years (N=57)	58	26	12	4
55 years or more (N=58)	55	32	16	7
Under $5,000 (N=22)	50	32	9	9
$5,000–$10,000 (N=66)	38	24	32	6
More than $10,000 (N=123)	58	24	17	1
Not a high-school graduate (N=31)	45	23	19	13
High-school graduate (N=56)	57	16	23	4
Some college education (N=52)	57	26	16	1
College graduate (N=58)	43	31	26	0
Democrat (N=154)	55	25	16	4
Republican (N=65)	48	20	31	2

variables were drastically reduced, with inter-family discussion showing the largest increase in activity. Like candidates, voters talked more as the campaign came to an end. Yet the association remained: the lower the income and formal education, the higher percentage of "no responses" to the question, "who do you most often talk with about politics?"

Income and Education

Income and education were also positively correlated with frequency of political discussions during the campaign: the higher the income and the greater the amount of formal education, the

more often voters talked politics with family, friends, or co-
workers (see Table 5–2). In Charlotte men voters engaged in
such political activity more often than women voters; younger
more often than older voters; and Republicans more often than
Democrats. These differences by sex, age, and party affiliation, as well as by income and education, remained intact even
when the salience of the campaign rose from June to October
and political talk among all citizen groupings increased. Men
also took a more active role in such political discussions than
did women (see Table 5–3). Neither age nor political affiliation
were good predictors of whether a person was more apt to listen or to talk and even try to convince others when politics was
the subject. But the correlation of both education and income

Table 5–2 Frequency of Political Discussion, by Sex, Age, Income, Education,
and Party Preference

Discussed Politics at least once a week	*In June (N=106)*	*In October (N=149)*
Total Sample (N=227)	47%	66%
Male (N=86)	56	73
Female (N=141)	41	61
Under 35 years (N=62)	55	76
35–44 years (N=50)	46	72
45–54 years (N=57)	46	61
55 years or more (N=58)	40	53
Under $5,000 (N=22)	32	55
$5,000–$10,000 (N=66)	39	64
More than $10,000 (N=123)	55	71
Not a high-school graduate (N=31)	26	45
High-school graduate (N=56)	41	61
Some college education (N=82)	46	68
College graduate (N=58)	64	78
Democrat (N=154)	44	64
Republican (N=65)	54	71

Table 5–3 Role During Discussions, by Sex, Age, Income, Education, Party Preference

	Mostly Listen	Talk/ Listen	Try to Convince	No Response
Total Sample (N=227)	49%	33%	13%	4%
Male (N=86)	40	38	19	4
Female (N=141)	55	29	9	4
Under 35 years (N=62)	48	42	7	3
35–44 years (N=50)	48	32	16	2
45–54 years (N=57)	53	26	18	2
55 years or more (N=58)	47	29	12	7
Under $5,000 (N=22)	55	27	9	5
$5,000–$10,000 (N=66)	53	33	3	11
More than $10,000 (N=123)	46	34	17	1
Not a high-school graduate (N=31)	45	26	7	13
High-school graduate (N=56)	59	32	5	2
Some college education (N=82)	51	31	15	4
College graduate (N=58)	38	40	21	2
Democrat (N=154)	50	33	12	4
Republican (N=65)	48	31	15	5

with the role taken in political discussions is striking. The majority of college graduates and those earning more than $10,000 a year admitted to expressing their own opinions and even trying to convince others on political matters, whereas only about a third of those with less than a high school education or making under $5,000 placed themselves in these more active political categories.

Using Media for Political News

The mounting interest of Charlotte voters in the election campaign, as evidenced by the increase from June to October in frequency of political discussions and type of participation in these discussions, was accompanied by greater use of the media for political news. This increase was due exclusively to the growing use of television for political news during the four-month period, so that the large newspaper lead over television in June disappeared by October.

Further indication of the rising interest in the campaign and in the issues associated with it is the greater disinclination by voters in October to accuse the press, including electronic journalism, of overkill; that is, of perceiving the press as paying "too much attention to some things." Moreover, the voters' need for more information about national issues did not diminish as summer gave way to fall, despite the growing volume of information processing in which they indulged during this period, both within their interpersonal networks and from the media networks. This informational need actually increased. Whereas only a few more than a third of the sample voters admitted in June that they did not have enough information about important issues more than half of them acknowledged such a need for more information in October. Probably it was the perception of need, as much as the need itself, which was growing. All of us know that intelligent voting requires information.

Political News and Political Discussion

The political use of both newspapers and television was positively associated with frequency of political discussion (see Table 5–4). This correlation between use of the two types of communication systems, interpersonal and press, by the Charlotte electorate was stronger in October than in June. A drop in amount of newspaper reading and a rise in amount of television viewing between the two measuring periods occurred for each type of political discussant.

Voters who discussed politics daily registered the sharpest increase in political viewing and the smallest decrease in political reading. For these daily discussants, the newspaper remained the more relied upon medium for political information, though by a much smaller margin than in June. The wide disparity in the political use of the two media noted in June for the three largest categories, with newspapers as tops for each type of voter, had all but vanished by October.

Table 5-4 Frequency of Political Discussion, by Media Use and by Information Factors

	In June			
	Never (N=20)	Occasionally (N=100)	Frequently* (N=64)	Daily (N=42)
Political use of papers "a great deal"	20%	51%	70%	74%
Political use of television "a great deal"	20	35	52	52
Need for information	40	48	33	33
Perceived media overkill	35	35	59	41

	In October			
	Never (N=9)	Occasionally (N=68)	Frequently* (N=85)	Daily (N=64)
Political use of papers "a great deal"	33%	43%	52%	72%
Political use of television "a great deal"	33	38	53	64
Need for information	22	62	46	53
Perceived media overkill	33	34	32	38

*Frequently = "once or twice a week."

Need for Information

Frequency of discussion was also correlated, but only slightly, with need for information and perceived overemphasis by the press, but this weak association seemed true only early in the campaign. That is, in June but not in October, the more often voters discussed politics, the more apt were they to perceive the press as paying too much attention to some issues and did not feel they needed more information. By October, however, all voters reported more need for information and fewer reported any sense of press overkill of political subjects (see Table 5–5). Furthermore those who reported they often tried to convert others to their political views reported increased use of both newspapers and television. Apparently they felt a need for up-to-date political ammunition.

Media Interest and Media Use

This analysis of some of the interpersonal dimensions of a citizen's involvement in a political campaign has not addressed itself directly to delineating the relationship between press exposure and participation in political discussions.

Specifically it does not decide between two important alternatives:

1. Did the press during the 1972 presidential campaign create or increase voters' interest in the campaign, leading them to engage in more political discussions and even to a more active role during such discussions, or

2. Did increased political activity on the interpersonal level, anticipated or actual, arouse a greater need for more political information, leading voters to use the readily accessible media?

Table 5-5 Usual Role in Political Discussions, by Media Use and Information Factors

Modal Role in Discussion:	Usually Listen (N=15)	Some Talk (N=96)	Talk/Listen (N=74)	Try to Convince (N=29)
Political use of papers "a great deal"				
in June	60%	51%	69%	66%
in October	53	52	53	72
Political use of television "a great deal"				
in June	47	35	53	38
in October	47	51	51	66
Need for information				
in June	40	44	39	35
in October	73	59	45	38
Perceived media overkill				
in June	27	42	42	59
in October	0	31	37	48
Discussion of politics at "least once a week"				
in June	13	31	66	86
in October	67	54	73	93

These findings suggest simultaneous use of both interpersonal and press networks for political information during the campaign by the Charlotte voters of both sexes, all ages, diverse economic standing, and educational background and political affiliation, although the degree of such use varied as we have seen.

More than a decade ago, such fusion of the private and public communication channels was designated by Lucian Pye as a characteristic trait of a modern society.[1] This fusion enhances the democratic political process—citizen participation in the public life of the community and of the nation. We watch, read, and listen, but we also talk and act.

Some differences among voters, however, strengthen the prospect that press effects may be discerned differently among voters according to the extent and nature of their involvement in interpersonal political networks.

Need for orientation, detailed in a later chapter, has been identified as an important psychological factor which leads to heavy use of the press and eventually to the appearance of the agenda-setting effect. The rationale linking the two levels of communication networks—press use and interpersonal talk—may be outlined in these propositions:

1. If the orientational need exists, information seeking follows.

2. The need for more information (currently the most common interpretation of "need for orientation") is strengthened by the perceived utility of information seeking.

3. Anticipated involvement in discussions on a particular subject with friends, co-workers, or family members provides such an incentive for seeking more information, especially if one is accustomed to or intends to join actively in the conversations. All of us want to be knowledgeable, or appear so.

4. If the interpersonal exchanges relate to public matters, the principal and most accessible source for such information in the technologically more advanced nations—Pye's "modern societies"—is the press.

An Agenda-Setting Hypothesis

Accordingly, during a presidential campaign when politics is a salient topic, the more frequent and active the participation in political discussions, the closer the personal agendas may resemble the media's agenda of national issues.

To test this hypothesis, the agenda of the sample of Charlotte voters was established with six of the seven "official" issues by the paired-comparison method.[2] With this restricted list of issues, support for agenda setting was found only for the newspaper, not for television, and then only as a cumulative effect.

The highest associations of the voter panel's aggregate agenda with that of the Charlotte *Observer* were achieved only when the paper's agenda over a four-month period, June through September, was used to compute the correlations. The month-by-month agendas of the local paper were insignificantly and at times somewhat negatively related to the voters' agenda. Apparently the press's agenda-setting effects on political cognitions is rather gradual. We read but we are not necessarily overwhelmed, most certainly not at once.

The analysis shown in Table 5–6 does not include television's contribution to agenda setting in Charlotte. The impact of television over time on voters could not be examined here because television news broadcasts were monitored only during June and October. Television data are dropped from the final analysis of this chapter.

Compared by frequency of personal discussion, voters are compared with the four-month *Observer* agenda for June and October in Table 5–6. In each comparison, the agenda-setting hypothesis is not substantiated for the earlier period of the campaign but is supported to varying degrees just before the election. This suggests that salience of the event may be a necessary condition for agenda setting to occur.

We should remember that use of the newspaper for political purposes slightly decreased by October for many voters. But the October agenda of the sample is not matched with the newspaper's monthly agenda (either September or October) but with its four-month June through September agenda. The cumulative impact of exposure to newspaper political coverage is thereby illustrated.

Nevertheless, except in one case, the agendas among the various voter subgroups are more closely aligned with each other than they are with the newspaper's agenda. This pattern favoring personal influence over press impact could be assessed casually as evidence against agenda setting. This would be a hasty and incorrect conclusion because issues, unlike men, are not created equal.

Some Issues Are More Important than Others

As measured by the paired-comparison method of ranking issues, Charlotte voters gave a high priority to the drug issue. (See Chapter Three for the ranking of this and other issues in response to an open-ended question.) Almost invariably, drugs appeared first or second for all types of voters examined here. This issue failed to reach a higher rank than fourth, and was

Table 5-6 Spearman's Rank-Order Correlations Among Agendas* of Political Discussants and Charlotte *Observer*

June Agendas

Frequency of Discussion	Seldom/Not at all	Frequently	Daily
Seldom or not at all			
Frequently	.83		
Daily	.94	.77	
Charlotte *Observer*	-.37	-.09	-.15

October Agendas

Frequency of Discussion			
Seldom or not at all			
Frequently	.83		
Daily	.94	.94	
Charlotte *Observer*	.26	.60	.54

Table 5-6 (cont'd)

June Agendas

Role in Discussion	Mostly Listen	Talk/Listen	Convince
Mostly listen			
Talk/listen	.94		
Try to convince	.94	1.00	
Charlotte Observer	−.37	−.26	−.26

October Agendas

Role in Discussion: Mostly listen			
Talk/listen	.83		
Try to convince	.77	.94	
Charlotte Observer	.89	.60	.54

*The voter issues are based on a paired-comparison system of ranking six of the "official agenda" items (see Appendix).

often fifth or last, in the Observer's agenda of six issues. A comparison of issue rankings between the Observer and voters indicates the widely divergent perception of the importance of the drug issue, an issue far more important to voters than press (as represented by amount of news devoted to the topic). This accounts for low correlations between these two agendas.

The drug issue may not have been perceived by most voters merely as one of several national problems but—and for many perhaps, chiefly—as a community or even family problem. In this study, the paired comparisons were introduced, albeit in the context of the political campaign, with the statement, "Different people are concerned with very different things . . . various issues or problems."

Perhaps in a conservative Southern community, respondents confronted with the pairing of a problem like drugs with issues more pertinent to the "distant" national campaign, are more likely to follow their personal saliences in reporting "which of the two (they) are more concerned about."

In the paired comparisons, Charlotte voters indicated by their overwhelming vote for drugs in June and again in October, that it was a primary concern. On a topic as personally salient as drugs, cues from the media evidently are not always needed.

If the issue of drugs is deleted from the list of ranked issues—leaving five more public issues—the correlations of the agendas for the various voter types and the *Observer* range from .80 to .90 (see Table 5-7). In four cases these correlations equal or surpass the correlations found earlier among the interpersonal voter types (see Table 5-6).

Even if the drugs issue is not removed, the agenda of those whose usual role in political discussions was that of listener compared closely with the *Observer* agenda, a .89 correlation, stronger than correlations with voters who claimed to discuss politics frequently or daily. These "mostly listen" voters were not heavy users of newspapers for political information. Apparently these voters are listening to those who do read and view the news, an example of indirect press influence.

Table 5-7 Spearman Rank-Order Correlations Between Political Discussants and *Observer* on Five-Item Agenda* in October

Frequency of Discussion		Role in Discussion	
Seldom or not at all	.85	Mostly listen	.80
Frequently	.80	Talk/listen	.80
Daily	.90	Try to convince	.90

*The issue of drugs is not included in this analysis.

Furthermore, if the drugs issue is dropped from the analysis, voters who engage in daily political discussions or who try to convert others to their views emerge with concerns which closely correlate with the *Observer*, .90, one of the highest agenda-setting correlations encountered in the entire Charlotte study.

Talk Versus Thought

These high correlations are striking because what is being compared with the newspaper's agenda in each case is not an *interpersonal* agenda of those involved in political discussions during the campaign, but their aggregate *intrapersonal* agenda: not necessarily what they said they talked about with others but what they said they personally thought were the most important issues.

This appears for the *Observer*'s agenda among those who characterize themselves as daily participants in political discussions, most of whom reported they "have definite ideas and try to convince" others who join them in talk about politics. These self-styled opinion leaders among Charlotte's registered voters had a political agenda that closely matched the *Observer*'s agenda. They may have been leaders but they were not alone.

Of course agenda setting can be indirect. The local paper may indirectly shape the priorities of even nonreaders if these nonreaders join group discussions or engage in political conversations which take their cue from the newspaper. The 52 Charlotte respondents who reported membership in organized groups "to which any of the six issues is important" more closely approximated the *Observer*'s agenda than did the majority of voters who were not affiliated with such organizations.[3]

But there is no intention here of invoking the mediating function of opinion leaders. The news relay process does not de-

mand opinion leaders as such. The topics and issues emphasized in the press can be introduced into a group discussion by
anyone in a group—leader or not—and may or may not be
picked up and elaborated upon by other, more prominent or re-
spected members of the group.

Media Use and Agenda Setting

Heavy media use, therefore, may not be a requirement for
agenda setting. Media impact on people's awareness of events
and issues, on their cognitive structures, on their determining
what is most relevant to a particular situation, like a political
campaign, may often be indirect.

But what people think about, the issues they personally are
most concerned about, need not be the same as what they talk
about, or listen to, during a political conversation.

Since the Charlotte study, it has been empirically established that intrapersonal and interpersonal agendas can differ
considerably and, when they do, what people think about
rather than what they talk about regarding public issues more
closely matches the priorities assigned to these issues by the
press.[4] This finding, coupled with the Charlotte evidence, suggests an intriguing possibility. It may be that interpersonal
agendas (the topics people talk about but are not necessarily
personally concerned about) are closely aligned with television's current news agenda, while interpersonal agendas
more closely resemble the newspaper's more extended news
priorities.

The issues voters are personally concerned about is apparently the result of a long, cumulative process as the Charlotte study evidence reveals—about four months. As has been
observed, "Discussions are usually topical; thinking need not
be."[5]

Competing Hypotheses

The hypothesis that participation in interpersonal communication is positively related to agenda setting has received some confirmation in the Charlotte study, despite occasionally ambiguous findings. Yet the exact nature and specific location of the interpersonal factors in the agenda-setting process remain unclear. Social utility (anticipated discussions for which one feels need for more information) may not be the primary explanation for the effects relationship between the two network levels.

Indeed, a contrary hypothesis is also plausible. Agenda setting is related negatively to frequency and degree of involvement in political discussions. Co-workers, friends, and family members also supply cues about what a voter should attend to. What wife or husband ignores each other, for very long? Interpersonal discussions can provide an alternative experience of political reality and the probability of an alternative agenda model. That often in fact these discussions do not provide this experience is evidence of the pervasive impact of the press upon us, not only for our individual cognitive structuring but also for our interpersonal communication behavior regarding public events and issues. In a modern society, widely different groups, both formal and informal, often use the press as a guide for establishing their own agendas. Thus it happens that a group setting may reinforce the press's agenda for us by providing occasions for political interchange on topics supplied by the press.

Whether this reinforcement approach or the social utility hypothesis argued by proponents of the press agenda-setting role will more precisely relate to interpersonal factors still must be determined. Clearly, however, both press and other people help shape our ideas. Only sometimes the press seems to shout a bit louder. Or perhaps it is only more repetitious.

NOTES

[1]Lucian W. Pye, "Models of Traditional, Transitional, and Modern Communication Systems," in Pye (ed.), *Communications and Political Development* (Princeton: Princeton University Press, 1963), pp. 24–29.

[2]Each voter determined in 15 separate comparisons which of the two issues he or she was more concerned about. The resulting relative scale values of concern for each of the six issues were converted into ordinal values to permit comparison with the press rankings of these issues. See Allen L. Edwards, *Techniques of Attitude Scale Construction* (New York: Appleton-Century-Crofts, 1957), pp. 19–52. The ordering of issues representing the "official" agenda used in other chapters was based upon a simple ranking of issues. Here the paired-compairson method was used in order to obtain a more rigorous ranking for intrapersonal comparisons. "Watergate/governmental corruption" was the only official agenda item not included in the paried comparisons (see Appendix).

[3]The *Observer*'s agenda of the six issues correlated .66 with the agenda of group-affiliated voters and .54 with nonmembers' agenda.

[4]See Jack McLeod, Lee B. Becker, and James E. Byrne, "Another Look at the Agenda-Setting Function of the Press," *Communication Research*, 1:131–41 (April 1974); and Maxwell McCombs, "A Comparison of Intra-Personal and Inter-Personal Agendas of Public Issues," Paper presented to the Political Communication Division, International Communication Association, April, 1974, New Orleans.

[5]Eugene F. Shaw, "Some Interpersonal Dimensions of the Media's Agenda-Setting Function," Paper presented at the Conference on the Media and the Agenda-Setting Function, October, 1974, Syracuse, New York.

*

Newspapers Versus Television: Mass Communication Effects Across Time

MAXWELL E. McCOMBS
Syracuse University

> *What happens—and what is written and broadcast—the day after a primary is more important than what happens at the polls.*
>
> David Broder, "Some Lessons From Past Presidential Years," Raleigh *News and Observer*, January 10, 1976

An agenda-setting function for mass communication means that the mass media influence voters' perceptions of what are the important issues. This is an assertion that the mass media are a major causal factor in shaping voters' personal assessments of what the key issues are in a political campaign.

The Charlotte study was designed with these causal questions about the agenda-setting function of mass communication explicitly in mind. To gain the key evidence on time-order, the sequence of events and agendas in the media and among the voters, the Charlotte survey was designed as a panel study in which the same random sample of voters was interviewed during June prior to the national political conventions, again in

October during the height of the campaign as President Nixon rolled toward victory, and finally in November after the Mc-Govern defeat.

Our immediate focus here will be on the months of June and October and the agendas of political issues presented by the Charlotte *Observer*, CBS, and NBC compared to the personal agendas of political issues of those voters who reported these news media as their primary and regular sources of political information.[1]

To ascertain the relationships between these mass media agendas and voter agendas across time, a series of cross-lagged correlational analyses was carried out. The primary advantage of cross-lagged correlations is that they provide direct evidence on the agenda-setting relationship across time, a major requisite for asserting that one agenda causes or influences another. The logic behind cross-lagged analysis is that if one variable really is the cause of another, the correlation of X (the cause) at time one with Y (the effect) at time two should be stronger than the opposite cross-lag, Y the effect at time one with the cause X at time two. Here the hypothesized X is the news media agenda and Y is the voter agenda. In all these analyses time one is June 1972 and time two is October 1972.

Cross-lagged analysis also has another advantage. There is a built-in alternative hypothesis. Here the agenda-setting hypothesis that "the media at time one influence voters at time two" is juxtaposed with the alternative hypothesis that "the voters at time one influence the press agenda at time two." In short, cross-lagged analysis comes closest to answering the old question: Which came first, the chicken or the egg?

The full array of information generated in each cross-lagged analysis is illustrated in Figure 6–1, which uses the agendas of the Charlotte *Observer* for June and October and the agendas for those same months of those voters who indicated that the *Observer* was the only newspaper they read. Our major concern is with the diagonal arrows in the figure. These are the arrows and correlations for the two alternative causal hypotheses. In this initial analysis the evidence is quite clear. The agenda-setting relationship (Newspaper at Time One corre-

lated with Voters at Time Two) is substantially stronger than
the alternative hypothesis (Voters at Time One correlated with
the Newspaper at Time Two). The rank-order correlations
(Spearman's rho) based on the seven key issues in 1972 are
+.51 versus +.19, a difference of .32 between the two.[2]

FIGURE 6–1

Cross-lagged Correlation Comparison of Charlotte Voters and the
Charlotte *Observer* in June and October 1972

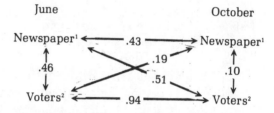

[1]Correlations are based on the "official" newspaper agenda.
[2]Analysis is based on panel members who read *only* the Charlotte *Observer*
(N=178).

Furthermore, this across-time correlation between the newspaper agenda and the voters' agenda is stronger than either of
the synchronous correlations between newspaper and voter
agendas. That is, the newspaper agenda of political issues in
June is a better predictor of the voters' agenda in October than
it is of the voters' agenda in June. Similarly, the June newspaper agenda is a better predictor than the October newspaper agenda of how the voters rank the issues in October.
These comparisons of the across-time agenda-setting correlations are further evidence of the causal influence of the media
on voters' perceptions of the key issues over time.

This evidence of the impact of the mass media over time on
issue salience among Charlotte voters in 1972 is strikingly similar to another pattern of cognitive impact among Wisconsin
adolescents during 1968. Researchers Steven Chaffee, Scott
Ward, and Leonard Tipton[3] also found in the Wisconsin study
stronger correlations across time than synchronously between
mass media exposure and political knowledge.

These two comparisons with the agenda-setting cross-
lagged correlation taken from Figure 6–1 are summarized in

the first line of Table 6–1. There we see that the agenda-setting cross-lag correlation coefficient does exceed the alternative cross-lag relationship (by +.32) and that the agenda-setting cross-lag coefficient also exceeds both of the synchronous agenda-setting coefficients, being .05 points more than the larger of the two static, synchronous correlations. Table 6–1 also summarizes the results of five additional cross-lagged analyses. These additional analyses examined the fit between the *Observer* and the *News* (line 4 in Table 6–1) and then introduced a control for how much each voter used newspapers to follow politics in the 1972 campaign.

In every case the agenda-setting influence of the press is demonstrated by the cross-lagged analyses. All six cross-lagged comparisons show sizable differences in the predicted direction. Partitioning the voters into two groups according to their extent of political information-seeking in the newspaper still sustains the agenda-setting hypothesis, but does demonstrate some tendency for low users to show a higher level of agreement with the newspapers' agenda over time.

The majority of analyses summarized in Table 6–1 also found the cross-lagged agenda-setting correlation to be stronger than any of the synchronous agenda-setting correlations. Only for "readers of both newspapers" (line 4) and "readers of both newspapers—high information-seekers" (line 6) was the agenda-setting cross-lag exceeded by the correlation between the newspaper and voters in June. None of the October newspaper-voter correlations was higher than the correlation over time.

TV as a News Source

Does the same pattern of agenda-setting hold for television news? Television has increasingly been touted and damned as the major influence in contemporary politics. Yet some of the preliminary findings from research on the agenda-setting function of mass communication done prior to the 1972 election suggest that TV does not exert a massive agenda-setting influence on the electorate. Here the cross-lagged analysis matched the

Table 6-1 Cross-lagged Correlation Comparison of Charlotte Voters and the Charlotte *Observer* in June and October 1972

Voter group	Is Newspaper → Voters > Voters → Newspaper?		Cross-lag > Synchronous	
Observer	Yes	+.32[1]	Yes	+.05
With control for use of newspaper to follow politics				
Low newspaper users	Yes	+.35[1]	Yes	+.03
High newspaper users	Yes	+.23	Yes	+.26
Readers of both newspapers	Yes	+.28[1]	No	−.11
With control for use of newspaper to follow politics				
Low newspaper users	Yes	+.60[1]	Yes	+.35
High newspaper users	Yes	+.17	No	−.12

[1]The Newspaper → Voter cross-lag exceeds the baseline correlation, while the Voter → Newspaper cross-lag does not. For details on computing the baseline (value expected by chance) see Leonard Tipton, Roger D. Haney, and John R. Baseheart, "Media Agenda-Setting in City and State Election Campaigns," Journalism Quarterly, 52:15-22 (Spring 1975).

CBS agenda in June and October against the agenda of voters who reported using CBS as their regular source of news. Then the same cross-lagged analysis was repeated for NBC and NBC viewers.

Unlike the analysis of newspaper influence across time, the television data do not yield any patterns of agenda-setting over the same period of time. None of the six cross-lags summarized in Table 6-2 supports the agenda-setting hypothesis. In every case the correlation of TV at Time One with Voters at Time Two is weaker than the obverse, Voters at Time One with TV at Time Two. Furthermore, in five of the six analyses the cross-lagged agenda-setting correlation is weaker than either of the synchronous same-time correlations between the voters' agenda and the TV agenda. For example, CBS in June correlates only +.30 with Voters in October. But in June the CBS/Voters correlation is +.32 and in October the match is +.77.

It also is instructive to examine the shift across time in the synchronous agenda-setting correlations. How does the match between the press and the voters' agenda in June compare with the match in October? For the Charlotte *Observer*, the synchronous match between the newspaper agenda and the voters' agenda declined over the summer months of 1972. While most of the declines are not large, nevertheless, the newspaper trends in Table 6–3 contrast strongly with the TV trends, which with a single exception are all positive. The increased correlation between the CBS agenda and the voters' agenda during the summer and early fall of 1972 is especially striking. This sharply increased agreement from June to Octo-

Table 6–2 Cross-lagged Correlation Comparison of Charlotte Voters and Various Television Network Agendas in June and October 1972

Voter group	Is TV → Voters > Voters→TV?		Cross-Lag > Synchronous	
CBS viewers	No	−.31[1]	No	−.02
With control for use of TV to follow politics				
Low users	No	−.44[1]	No	−.01
High users	No	−.14[3]	Yes	+.25[2]
NBC viewers	No	−.52[1]	No	−.20
With control for use of TV to follow politics				
Low users	No	−.53[1]	No	−.20
High Users	No	−.42[1]	No	−.08

[1] The Voter → TV cross-lag exceeds the baseline correlation, while the TV → Voter (agenda-setting) cross-lag does not.

[2] While the CBS/voters cross-lag exceeded the June synchronous correlation by +.25, it is .11 lower than the October synchronous correlation.

[3] Both cross-lag correlations exceed the baseline.

ber between CBS and its viewers in Charlotte on ranking the
major issues in the campaign did not result from extensive
treatment of the Watergate scandal by CBS. In the CBS coverage Watergate and related affairs moved from sixth place to
third from June to October. But among those voters in Charlotte
who viewed the CBS news regularly, Watergate held steady in
fourth place on their agenda of issues. Rather than Watergate,
the increased match resulted from greater agreement on the
ranking of three lesser issues, the environment, relations with
Russia and China, and the drug problem. These are termed
lesser issues because their mean rankings both by CBS and the
voters were five or lower in both June and October.

Table 6-3 Changes in the Synchronous Correlations between the Voters'
Agenda and Media Agenda from June to October 1972

Analysis	Change
Observer	−.36
With control for use of newspaper to follow politics	
Low newspaper users	−.18
High newspaper users	−.22
Readers of both newspapers	−.13
With control for use of newspaper to follow politics	
Low newspaper users	−.03
High newspaper users	−.14
CBS viewers	+.45
With control for use of TV to follow politics	
Low users	+.53
High users	+.36
NBC viewers	+.21
With control for use of TV to follow politics	
Low users	−.09
High users	+.27

In view of the striking contrasts between the newspaper and
TV, both in the pattern of influence across time and the pattern
of change in the synchronous agenda-setting correlations, it is
especially interesting to find a replication of these patterns in a
study by Leonard Tipton et al of agenda-setting in a state election. Their study also found an agenda-setting effect across
time for newspapers, but not television. Furthermore, the synchronous agenda-setting correlations for TV showed the same
increase over time. The newspaper synchronous pattern is
mixed in their study, showing an increase in one instance and a
decrease in another.[4]

The Agenda-Setting Process

There seem to be distinct agenda-setting roles for newspapers
and television, at least as the media fulfilled these roles in
Charlotte during the 1972 presidential campaign. The newspaper showed a stronger initial match with the voters' issue
concerns in June that did the two TV networks. And, from June
until October, the newspaper agenda showed more influence
on the voter concerns expressed in October. Despite these
early advantages for the newspaper in wielding agenda-setting
influence, by October voter concerns showed a better match
with TV than with the newspaper.

Was it a matter of "TV catching up" with the newspaper and
the public? For the newspapers the available evidence clearly
says "No!" A cross-lagged correlation analysis of newspaper
content and TV content in June and October shows no indication of any newspaper influence on the TV agenda. There is no
evidence for any agenda-setting within the media or any two-
step flow of issue salience from the newspaper to television.

For the public, the answer is, at least partially, "Yes." The
cross-lagged analyses summarized in Table 6–2 clearly indicate public influence on the TV agendas across time. In other
words, these media *catch up with, adjust their agenda to fit the*

agenda of their audience. By October the TV networks are better attuned to their audiences' agenda, more so in fact than is the newspaper. These increased levels of agreement might result simply from feedback, but the superiority of the TV correlations also suggests some TV agenda-setting influence in the final weeks of the campaign.

In short, the Charlotte data describe two distinct phases in agenda-setting. In the early precampaign period and as the campaign begins, the prime mover is the newspaper alone. But as we move into the campaign period itself, this influence of the press which has built up across time is shared with television. Given the rather low correlations between the content of the various media during October, it is a matter of sharing rather than reinforcement.

These differences in the agenda-setting roles of newspapers and television stem, in part, from basic differences in the two media of communication. A medium of communication is influenced by technology, and technological constraints are imposed upon the journalist who uses a particular medium. The original McCombs and Shaw 1968 agenda-setting study documented technological constraints on the agenda of public issues reported by each news medium. While there were some parallels among the agendas of all the news media—parallels imposed by social realities and common journalistic norms —each medium was most like those other media sharing the same technology. Each newspaper's agenda of public issues was more like the agenda of other newspapers than television. Each television network's agenda of public issues was more like the agenda of other TV networks than newspapers.

Medium Shapes the Message

The medium shapes the message, and the medium shapes the social role of the message. Newspapers perform more of an initiating role in public opinion than does television. With their greater channel capacity—dozens and dozens of pages in contrast to a half hour for most TV news presentations—newspapers can pick up public issues at an earlier point in their life cycle. An emerging issue can be given occasional space in the back pages of the newspaper. TV news is more like the front page. Only when issues have achieved prominence are they likely to rate TV news time or front page space.

Because of this ability to begin tracking and reporting public issues earlier, newspapers play the lead role in initial presentation of issues to the public. Our study documents this role of the newspaper during the 1972 presidential campaign in Charlotte.

Television—an entirely different technology—plays a separate social role. Something about this audio-visual medium of communication gives it almost universal appeal. Television may be the ultimate mass medium. It attunes a larger audience to the political campaign, making politics salient to many voters unreached by the newspaper. Not only does television broaden the base of the interested electorate and raise the level of salience of politics in society as the campaign progresses, television also influences and shapes the public agenda.

As we have seen, television does not mimic the newspaper agenda. Television news cuts into reality at a different angle. It is, for one, more visually oriented. Television news also has a very different style from news stories in the print media. TV news is not newspaper news with pictures.

In short, the two news media play distinct roles in the shaping of the public agenda. Because of technological differences, newspapers take the lead during the first phase. But in a second phase they share the stage, and TV with its wide appeal dominates. Since there are stylistic as well as technological dissimilarities between the two communication media, this later phase in agenda-setting is a matter of sharing rather than reinforcement.

The Nature of
Agenda-Setting

So far we have always spoken simply of an agenda, be it a voter agenda or a mass media agenda, or of agenda-setting. But there are many ways to describe an agenda or an agenda-setting influence. Perhaps the major advance in our understanding of the agenda-setting process can be described by three distinct models of what we mean by agenda-setting.

The simplest version can be called the 0/1 or *awareness* model. Here the question is simply one of awareness versus ignorance. This basic, primitive notion of agenda-setting is a truism. If the media tell us nothing about a topic or event, then in most cases it simply will not exist on our personal agendas or in our life space. To a considerable degree, especially in the realm of public affairs, only items communicated by the media can appear on personal agendas. In this simple 0/1 situation there necessarily is significant linkage between media and personal agendas, especially for items outside the immediate environment.

The concept of agenda-setting—especially as empirically developed—urges a more detailed model: 0/1/2..N, namely that among the many topics or attributes transmitted by the media, the same basic distinctions as to priorities will be transferred from the media agenda to the individual's agenda. More simply it amounts to this: we judge as important what the media judge important. The media's priorities become our own.

It really is this bolder hypothesis emphasized in most of the research to date. Not merely the appearance or nonappearance of the message is important in agenda-setting, though that certainly is. But such characteristics as display and position—page one versus inside, top of the page versus bottom, large headline versus small headline—and sheer length are key attributes of the stimulus presented to the audience. And, following the basic assumption of quantitative content analysis, the sheer frequency of appearance of the stimulus is an important aspect of the learning process.

Now there is, of course, a very finite limit to how far this priorities model can be extended. A lengthy set of media priorities (say a dozen or more topics) is unlikely to be directly translated into a highly similar set of personal priorities by the audience. For example, a lengthy list of legislative concerns (about two dozen covered in the press) showed no correlation with the priorities of members of the state legislature. But when that set was reduced to a half dozen broad topics, then there was considerable overlap between the media agenda and the personal agendas of the legislators.[5]

Somewhere around five, six, or seven is the likely cutoff point for this 0/1/2..N model of agenda-setting. It is the magic number seven plus or minus two revisited. As you recall, psychologist George Miller found that seven was the finite limit to a number of psychological phenomena involving span of attention.[6]

Something in this range also is the likely limit to the size of most personal agendas. People concentrate on a small number of social priorities, not the dozens of topics that appear daily in the press.

Intermediate between the 0/1 awareness and the 0/1/2..N priority models is an agenda-setting effect we might label *salience*. This is the 0/1/2 model. Heavy media emphasis on an issue or topic can move it above threshold and into the top ranks of the personal agendas of the audience. This occurs only for a few items constantly emphasized in the media. This version of agenda-setting extends beyond simple awareness. A discrimination is made by the audience as to high and low importance of items, but the exact priorities of the media are not reproduced within personal agendas. In short, the media may influence saliences, but not exact priorities.

Obviously, the three models of agenda-setting effects outlined here—awareness, salience, and priorities—are cumulative. Each adds subsequent precision and detail to those preceding it. And, as indicated, the priorities model probably is limited to about seven items. So we have a range of agenda-setting effects. It is not a matter of deciding which model is correct. To some degree they all are. The task before us now is to explicate the situations in which each of these agenda-setting models provides the best perspective for detailing the role of mass communication.

Comparing the Salience and Priorities Models

Since the awareness model is a truism, the focus here is on a comparison of the salience and priorities models. Which concept is a better description of the match between voter agendas and mass media agendas?

To make this comparison we need two kinds of information from each voter. First, a standardized list of individual priorities which can be compared to the news media agenda is needed for an operational definition of the priorities model. Fortunately, the questionnaire used in Charlotte during the 1972 campaign included a set of six issues presented to the survey respondents as paired-comparisons, a set of 15 pairs containing all possible combinations of the six issues (see Appendix). For each pair the respondent indicated which issue was most important to him or her. Each issue thus had a score ranging from 0 (meaning that the issue was never selected as most important regardless of what it was paired with) to 5 (meaning that the issue was always selected as most important regardless of what it was paired with). On the basis of these scores it was possible to construct a rank-ordering for each voter and compare (correlate) this rank-ordering with a news medium's rank-ordering of the same issue. High rank-order correlations would be evidence of a good fit to the priorities model; low correlations, evidence of a bad fit to the priorities model.

For the salience model the same data were organized in a simpler fashion. Vietnam was the number one media issue throughout the 1972 campaign. If a survey respondent's highest issue score from the set of paired-comparisons was for Vietnam, then his or her match with the press was operationally defined as demonstrating a good fit to the salience model. If another issue had a higher score, his or her match with the press was operationally defined as demonstrating a bad fit to the salience model.

In short, it is possible to simultaneously classify the match between each voter's agenda and a news medium's agenda as showing good or bad fits to both the salience and priorities models. As Figure 6–2 shows this yields four possibilities: one situation where only the salience model shows a good fit, one where only the priorities model shows a good fit, one where both fit, and one where neither fits. The empirical question is where do most of the agenda-setting scores fall in this typology?

FIGURE 6–2

Cell Entries Indicate which Model Provides the Best Description of the Match Between Voter and Media Agendas

		Salience Model	
		Good	Bad
Priorities Model	Good	Both Models	Priorities Model
	Bad	Salience Model	Neither Model

Eight replications of this typology can be obtained from the 1972 Charlotte study. In addition to using the issue scores from the paired-comparisons for the respondent portion of the salience model description, a second measure is available: an open-ended question asking voters what issue or problem they were most concerned about.

If the respondent answered "Vietnam," there is a good salience model fit. If another issue was named, there is a poor salience model fit with the press agenda. Availability of these two different respondent agenda measures and two news media agendas (newspapers and television) to compare with during two different times (June and October) yields eight possible combinations (2 × 2 × 2) or replications. What does all this evidence mean?

The Empirical Scorecard

First, it should be noted in Table 6–4 that about four out of ten agenda-setting scores do not match either pattern. This is not unexpected. It has been repeatedly emphasized that agenda-setting influence is far from universal. Having again documented this point, let us compare the remaining three columns in Table 6–4.

Using the same data (the paired-comparison scores) to describe voters in salience and priority terms, which model describes the greater number of voters?

The largest group of voters in both June and October—about one-third of all the Charlotte voters interviewed—are accurately described by both models. Their individual correla-

Table 6–4 Four Comparisons of the Descriptive Power of the Priority and Salience Models Based on the Fit of Newspaper and Voter Agendas*

Source of Respondents' Agendas		Model Best Describing Agenda Match-up			
		Both	Priority	Salience	Neither
June	Paired-comparisons	32.8%	18.5	8.4	40.3
	Open-ended Q and Paired-comparisons	10.1%	42.2	5.5	42.2
October	Paired-comparisons	36.4%	14.5	6.8	42.3
	Open-ended Q and Paired-comparisons	16.5%	34.5	4.5	44.5

*Only the data based on the voter – newspaper agenda matches is displayed here since the TV agendas yielded an identical pattern. The average discrepancy was only 1.47 percent between the percentages in these four replications and the four TV replications.

tions with the media agendas (our measure of priorities) are high and they agree with the media in naming Vietnam as the single most important issue (our measure of salience).

Focusing on the two remaining groups—voters accurately described by only one model—the findings clearly favor the priorities model by a ratio of two-to-one.

Overall then, in both June and October, over half the agenda-setting scores are accurately described by the priorities model. About four out of ten are accurately described by the salience model, but this is no greater than the number not described by either agenda-setting model.

When different data are used to measure the two models (an open-ended question for the voter data for the salience model and paired-comparison scores for the voter data for the priorities model), which model most accurately describes the greater number of voters? (Again the "Neither" group in Table 6–4 has been set aside.)

Here the priorities model gains support, both in the comparison of agenda-setting scores described accurately by only one model and in the comparison including voters accurately described by both. Changing the technique of measurement used to obtain voter agendas does not alter the proportion of agenda-setting patterns accurately described by the salience model alone, it is still less than one in ten.

But the proportion of patterns accurately described by both models declines drastically and the proportion best described by the priorities model sharply increases. In a direct comparison of the priorities and salience models, the priorities model advances from the two-to-one ratio reported above to an eight-to-one ratio.

Overall, again in both June and October the match of over half of the Charlotte voters with the newspaper agenda is best described by the priorities model. With the shift to an open-ended measure of voter salience, the salience model does not do half as well as the priorities model in describing the agenda-setting relationship in Charlotte.

In short, the evidence clearly favors the more radical notion of agenda-setting, the priorities model, which asserts that the priorities of the media are transferred largely intact onto the public agenda. This finding that the priorities model is the more accurate description of agenda-setting patterns replicates across two methodologies, two news media, and two points in time.

NOTES

[1] ABC and the Charlotte *News* are omitted from the analyses presented here because too few voters indicated these as primary or regularly used sources of news. The Charlotte *News* is indirectly included, however, in the comparison of the Charlotte *Observer* agenda with the agenda of those voters who read both the *Observer* and *News* on a regular basis.

[2] While the "n" used to calculate the rank-order correlations is only 7, the number of major issues on the agenda, the correlation coefficients are far more stable than this n suggests because the issue rankings are based on the responses of 178 voters and over 200 newspaper items in each month analyzed. In short, the 7 issues are observation points at which data on large numbers of cases (voters or news stories) are aggregated.

[3] Steven H. Chaffee, L. Scott Ward, and Leonard P. Tipton, "Mass Communication and Political Socialization," *Journalism Quarterly*, 47:647–659, 666 (Winter 1970).

[4] Leonard Tipton, Roger D. Haney, and John R. Baseheart, "Media Agenda-setting in City and State Election Campaigns," *Journalism Quarterly*, 52:15–22 (Spring 1975).

[5] W. T. Gormley, "Newspaper Agendas and Political Elites," *Journalism Quarterly*, 52:304–308 (Summer 1975).

[6] George A. Miller, "The Magic Number Seven, Plus or Minus Two: Some Limits on Our Capacity for Processing Information," *Psychological Review*, 63:81–97 (March 1956).

*

Political Issues and Voter Need for Orientation

DAVID H. WEAVER
Indiana University

> *A desire of knowledge is the natural feeling of mankind.* . . .
>
> Dr. Samuel Johnson

It seems obvious that if mass communication is to have a direct agenda-setting impact on voters, voters must first be exposed to the message. Although this exposure may at times be accidental or incidental (especially in the case of broadcast media, billboards, and 72-point banner headlines), much of it is undoubtedly purposive, planned behavior. Therefore, one of the first questions to be addressed in the search for psychological explanations for agenda-setting is: Why do some voters expose themselves to certain mass media messages more than do other voters?

Although there is no single satisfactory answer, or set of answers, to this question, there are studies which shed some light in this area. In general, these studies indicate that three major factors (among many minor factors) play an important part in determining the messages to which a person will attend and how much of these messages he or she will perceive.

These factors are the degree of (1) *interest* in the message content; (2) *uncertainty* about the subject of the message; and (3) *effort required* to attend to the message (including the perceived likelihood that a reliable source of information is available). Obviously these are not final explanations because we may still ask why some people are more interested in, or more uncertain about, certain messages than are others, but these are starting points in the search for psychological explanations of agenda-setting.

McCombs and Weaver have incorporated the first and second of these psychological factors in their concept of need for orientation.[1] This concept assumes that each person feels some need to be familiar with his surroundings, both his physical and mental environment. According to Tolman's concept of cognitive mapping, each individual will strive to map his world, to fill in enough detail to orient himself, to intellectually find his way around.[2]

The importance of a need for orientation and the use of mass communication in fulfilling this need is documented in other studies. Westley and Barrow[3] and McCombs,[4] found that different levels of need for orientation accounted for the varying "effectiveness" of newspaper editorial endorsements in selected California political contests. Mueller,[5] who studied a Los Angeles junior college board election (with 133 candidates) where the usual orienting cues of party affiliation and incumbency were unavailable, found that four cues, including endorsement by the Los Angeles *Times*, were used by voters for orientation and accounted for the majority of differences in votes.

In short, McCombs and Weaver suggest that increased need for orientation leads to increased mass media use, which in turn leads to increased agenda-setting effects by media. As an individual strives to map political (or other) issues through the use of mass media, he is more susceptible (at least in many situations) to the agenda-setting effects of the media.

A Typology of Orientational Need

McCombs and Weaver use two factors to define need for orientation: (1) relevance of information and (2) degree of uncertainty concerning the subject of the message. Because the news media (newspapers and television in particular) permeate nearly every aspect of American life and are readily available to most citizens, the third factor suggested by studies of information seeking (degree of effort required to attend to the message) was taken as a given. Political information is certainly not hard to obtain, so the typology constructed depicts different levels of need for orientation by the differing amounts of relevance and uncertainty, as the following shows:

FIGURE 7-1

Antecedents of Need for Orientation

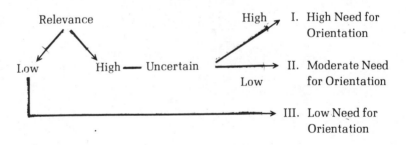

In this typology it is asserted that low relevance (regardless of degree of uncertainty) results in a low need for orientation (Group III), that high relevance and low uncertainty result in a moderate need for orientation (Group II), and that high relevance and high uncertainty result in a high need for orientation (Group I).

McCombs and Weaver also suggest that persons with a high need for orientation about political matters (Group I) are more susceptible to mass media agenda-setting influence with re-

gard to national political news issues than are Group II respon-
dents (those with a moderate need for orientation), and Group
II respondents are more susceptible to agenda-setting than
Group III respondents (those with a low need for orientation).

Recent Follow-up Findings

Complete data from the Charlotte study show that even when
relevance and uncertainty are measured in a number of ways,
differing levels of need for orientation are related systematically to frequency of use of mass media and to the strength of
the agenda-setting effect. In addition, these data lend support
to the predictive and explanatory value of simultaneously con-
sidering several factors such as relevance and uncertainty.

To measure relevance of politics to Charlotte voters, five
scales were used (three in June and two in October). To measure each respondent's degree of uncertainty about politics,
four scales were used (two in June and two in October).[6] In general, measures of relevance were gauges of political involvement (political interest, amount of political discussion or participation, and sense of effectiveness and commitment). Political uncertainty was measured by the degree of professed political party affiliation and firmness of choice of political candidate.

Need for Orientation
and Media Use

Use of political involvement to measure relevance of politics is
obvious. Use of party identification plus certainty of voting
choice to measure political uncertainty is based on the frequent finding that party identification is a major determinant
of the vote and, therefore, is a major orienting cue for voters.

In the absence of strong party identification and support of friends and family, the independent voter is deprived of a convenient orienting cue and thus has a high degree of uncertainty as he faces the task of choosing a candidate.

As Table 7–1 indicates, the prediction that Group I (those with a high need for orientation) will have a greater proportion of frequent media users than Group II (moderate need) is supported in 16 of 20 comparisons.[7] The prediction that Group II will have a larger proportion of frequent media users than Group III (low orientational need) is supported in 19 of 20 comparisons and the prediction that Group I will have a larger proportion of frequent media users than Group III is supported in all 20 comparisons. Overall, 55 of 60 possible comparisons among the three groups (91.7%) support the prediction that higher levels of need for orientation are associated with higher levels of mass media use.

Need for Orientation and Agenda-Setting

Need for orientation also is related to the agenda-setting effect of mass media, although less strongly and less systematically than to frequency of media use. Table 7–2 presents the rank-order correlation coefficients between the agendas of the various groups and the "official" agenda of the *Observer* for June.

Although these correlations with the *Observer* are not especially strong, Group I's agenda is more similar to the *Observer* agenda than is Group II's agenda in three of six comparisons, and Group II's agenda more closely resembles the newspaper agenda than Group III's agenda in five of six comparisons. In addition, Group I's agenda is more similar to the newspaper agenda than Group III's in all six comparisons. In short, 14 of the 18 possible comparisons among the three

Table 7-1 Need for Orientation and Frequent Use of Mass Media

Need For Orientation		A	B	C	D	E	Uncertainty Scales
Hi	I	79.8%*	65.6%	68.3%	68.0%	67.3%	(W)
Mod	II	62.5	64.3	74.2	73.1	76.2	
Lo	III	47.4	60.8	57.0	56.8	58.7	
	I	72.3	60.7	74.3	69.2	72.7	(X)
	II	69.2	64.6	66.1	65.3	61.8	
	III	46.2	57.6	54.0	54.1	56.4	
	I	84.8	70.0	72.4	71.0	75.0	(Y)
	II	66.0	61.6	68.2	65.0	62.5	
	III	46.2	57.9	54.0	54.5	56.7	
	I	81.0	80.0	78.9	74.2	68.4	(Z)
	II	69.4	54.5	68.4	63.2	68.0	
	III	43.1	59.3	53.2	53.8	57.8	
Relevance Scales		(A)	(B)	(C)	(D)	(E)	

*Indicates that 79.8 percent of the respondents in Group I (those with a high need for orientation) were frequent users of mass media (newspapers, television, and news magazines) for political information; 62.5 percent of the respondents in Group II (those with a moderate need for orientation) were frequent users of mass media; and 47.4 percent of the respondents in Group III (those with a low need for orientation) were frequent users of mass media.

Note: Two measures are needed to define an individual's level of need for orientation: a measure of relevance and a measure of uncertainty. To strengthen the analysis in this table a number of different measures are used to operationalize the two concepts defining need for orientation.

Specifically, the five measures of relevance are: (A) the political interest index; (B) political discussion index; (C) political participation index; (D) political efficacy scale; and (E) sense of citizen duty scale.

The four measures of uncertainty are: (W) strength of political party affiliation; (X) congruity of friends' perceived vote intention; (Y) congruity of family's perceived vote intention; and (Z) degree of certainty about choice of a presidential candidate to vote for.

Table 7-2 Need for Orientation and Newspaper Agenda-Setting (June 1972)

Need For Orientation				Uncertainty Scales
Hi	I .51*	I .29	I .35	
Mod	II .33	II .37	II .58	(W)
Lo	III .25	III .25	III .19	
	I .41	I .58	I .41	
	II .35	II .26	II .47	(Z)
	III .15	III .37	III .21	
Relevance Scales	(A)	(B)	(D)	

*Indicates that the agenda of national issues considered most important by Group I respondents (those with a high need for orientation) was correlated .51 (Kendall's tau) with the "official agenda" of national issues from the Charlotte Observer in June, 1972; that the agenda of Group II respondents (those with a moderate need for orientation) was correlated .33 with the newspaper agenda for June; and that the agenda of Group III respondents (those with a low need for orientation) was correlated .25 with the newspaper agenda for June.

Note: Two measures are needed to define an individual's level of need for orientation; a measure of relevance and a measure of uncertainty. To strengthen the analysis in this table a number of different measures are used to operationalize the two concepts defining need for orientation.

See Table 7-1 for the list of specific indicators.

groups (77.8%) support the positive relationship between need for orientation and susceptibility to the agenda-setting effect of newspapers.

Table 7-3 presents the rank-order correlation coefficients between the agendas of the various groups and the combined agenda of ABC, CBS, and NBC nightly national news broadcasts in June.[8] Although these correlations are generally not as strong as those involving the *Observer* agenda, they also indicate a positive relationship between need for orientation and the agenda-setting effect of television.

Group I's agenda is more closely related to the combined television agenda in three of six comparisons with group II; Group II's agenda more closely resembles the combined televi-

Table 7-3 Need for Orientation and Television Agenda-Setting (June 1972)

Need For Orientation				Uncertainty Scales
Hi	I .25*	I .24	I .29	
Mod	II .26	II .31	II .39	(W)
Lo	III .19	III 0	III .14	
	I .35	I .39	I .55	
	II .19	II .05	II .41	(Z)
	III 0	III .10	III .05	
Relevance Scales	(A)	(B)	(D)	

*Indicates that the agenda of national issues considered most important by Group I respondents (those with a high need for orientation) was correlated .25 (Kendall's tau) with the combined "official agenda" of issues from ABC, CBS, and NBC nightly news television broadcasts in June 1972; that the agenda of Group II respondents (those with a moderate need for orientation) was correlated .26 with the combined TV agenda; and that the agenda of Group III respondents (those with a low need for orientation) was correlated .19 with the combined TV agenda.

Note: Two measures are needed to define an individual's level of need for orientation; a measure of relevance and a measure of uncertainty. To strengthen the analysis in this table a number of different measures are used to operationalize the two concepts defining need for orientation.

See Table 7-1 for the list of specific indicators.

sion agenda than Group III's in five of six comparisons; and Group I's agenda is more similar to the television agenda than the agenda of Group III in all six comparisons. Overall, 14 of 18 comparisons (77.8%) support the prediction that voters with a higher need for orientation will be more susceptible to the agenda-setting effect of television than those with a lower need for orientation.

Closer to Election Time

Table 7-4 illustrates the rank-order correlations between the agendas of the different voter groups and the *Observer* for October, as the campaign came to a close. In October, 8 of 12 comparisons (66.7%) support a positive relationship between need for orientation and a newspaper agenda-setting effect.

Less support for a positive relationship between need for orientation and a television agenda-setting effect is presented in Table 7-5.[9] For television in October, only 4 of 12 comparisons (33.3%) support a positive correlation between voter need for orientation and the agenda-setting effect of television for October, a far weaker relationship than was true for the newspaper comparisons.

Table 7-4 Need for Orientation and Newspaper Agenda-Setting (October 1972)

Need For Orientation			Uncertainty Scales
Hi	I .68*	I .16	
Mod	II .59	II .24	(X)
Lo	III .29	III .33	
	I .58	I .51	
	II .52	II .19	(Y)
	III .29	III .33	
Relevance Scales	(C)	(E)	

Indicates that the agenda of national issues considered most important by Group I respondents (those with a high need for orientation) was correlated .68 (Kendall's tau) with the "official agenda" of the Observer in October 1972; that the agenda of Group II respondents (those with a moderate need for orientation) was correlated .59 with the Observer agenda; and that the agenda of Group III respondents (those with a low need for orientation) was correlated .29 with the Observer agenda.

Note: *Two measures are needed to define an individual's level of need for orientation: a measure of relevance and a measure of uncertainty. To strengthen the analysis in this table a number of different measures are used to operationalize the two concepts defining need for orientation.*

See Table 7-1 for the list of specific indicators.

Table 7-5 Need for Orientation and Television Agenda-Setting
(October 1972)

Need For Orientation				Uncertainty Scales
Hi	I .59*		I .27	
Mod	II .49		II .24	(X)
Lo	III .49		III .52	
	I .37		I .28	
	II .52		II .29	(Y)
	III .49		III .52	
Relevance Scales	(C)		(E)	

*Indicates that the agenda of national issues considered most important by
Group I respondents (those with a high need for orientation) was correlated .59 (Kendall's tau) with the combined "official agenda" of issues
from ABC, CBS, and NBC nightly news television broadcasts in October
1972; that the agenda of Group II respondents (those with a moderate
need for orientation) was correlated .49 with the combined TV agenda;
and that the agenda of Group III subjects (those with a low need for orientation) was correlated .49 with the combined TV agenda.

Note: Two measures are needed to define an individual's level of need for
orientation: a measure of relevance and a measure of uncertainty. To
strengthen the analysis in this table a number of different measures are
used to operationalize the two concepts defining need for orientation.

See Table 7-1 for the list of specific indicators.

Implications for Voting

How does this affect voting behavior and the outcome of elections? For voters with a strong party or candidate preference—those with low or moderate need for orientation—it
probably means what already has been found in research on
politics and the press: issue and candidate information most often reinforces our intentions to vote in line with our preferred
party and candidate.

Reinforcement is the opposite of change and some have pointed to this alleged ability of the press to cement our views in place and concluded that the press has little effect in changing our views.[10]

Yet this view ignores voters who are highly interested in politics and undecided about how to vote. In short they as yet have no views to cement in place. The close 1960 presidential election furthermore showed us that it does not take many of these people to determine the direction of a national election.

Voters and Issues

DeVries and Tarrance argue there is a growing number of persons who split party tickets in voting and that these ticket-splitters are a younger, educated group who use media more than most other people.[11] If so, these may be the very voters who can tip an election one way or another; at the same time these voters potentially are most susceptible to an agenda-setting influence of mass media.

This appears to mean that for voters with a high need for orientation about politics, mass media do more than merely reinforce. In fact, mass media may teach these voters the issues and topics to use in evaluating certain candidates and parties, not just during political campaigns, but also in the longer periods between campaigns.

One timely example of this teaching function can be seen in the heavy coverage given the Watergate scandal during the period between the 1972 presidential election and the 1974 gubernatorial and senatorial elections. By keeping this issue at the top of the news agenda for so many months, news media in effect told many voters it was an important criterion for judging political parties and candidates, even after President Nixon resigned in August 1974, three months before the fall elections. The dramatic Democratic wins in these elections at least in part may be interpreted as a testament to the agenda-setting

power of the press and relative impotency of short-term editorial endorsements and political campaigns.

   If voters highly interested and highly uncertain about which
party or candidate to support are most susceptible to media
news emphasis, this places a great responsibility on reporters
not just to report certain politically-related events and issues
as fairly as possible, but also to choose which events and issues
to cover with just as much fairness.

NOTES

[1]Maxwell E. McCombs and David H. Weaver, "Voters' Need for Orientation and Use of Mass Communication," Unpublished report prepared for presentation to International Communication Association, Montreal, Canada, 1973.

[2]Edward C. Tolman, *Purposive Behavior in Animals and Men* (New
   York: Appleton-Century, 1932).

[3]Bruce H. Westley and Lee Barrow, "An Investigation of News Seeking Behavior," *Journalism Quarterly*, 36:431–38 (Fall 1959).

[4]Maxwell E. McCombs, "Editorial Endorsements: A Study of Influence," *Journalism Quarterly*, 44:545–48 (Autumn 1967).

[5]John E. Mueller, "Choosing Among 133 Candidates," *Public Opinion
   Quarterly*, 34:395–402 (Fall 1970).

[6]Actual questions are in the Appendix. The political interest index
   was constructed from two variables: interest in the presidential
   campaign in June and concern over the outcome of the presidential
   campaign in June. These variables were summed because they
   loaded highly on one factor (.66 and .67 respectively) and negligibly
   on all other factors when factor analyzed with other variables, using a principal components method with varimax rotation.

   The political discussion index was formed by summing two June variables: frequency of discussion of specific political issues and frequency of discussion of politics in general. These variables loaded

.74 and .84 on one factor and negligibly on the others, using principal components factor analysis with varimax rotation.

[7]Frequency of mass media use for political information was measured in all instances by a Guttman quasi-scale composed of three variables: frequency of newspaper use for news about political candidates and issues, frequency of television viewing of news about political candidates and issues, and whether or not the respondent subscribed to a news magazine. Coefficient of reproducibility for the scale was .88 and coefficient of scalability was .65.

[8]The June 1972 agendas of ABC, CBS, and NBC nightly news broadcasts were combined into one TV agenda because of their high rank-order correlation (.96 between ABC and CBS, .57 between ABC and NBC, and .61 between CBS and NBC, all measured by Spearman's Rho).

[9]The October 1972 agendas of ABC, CBS, and NBC nightly news broadcasts were combined into one TV agenda because of their high rank-order correlation (.89 between ABC and CBS, .64 between ABC and NBC, and .75 between CBS and NBC, all measured by Spearman's Rho. See Chapter 3).

[10]Maxwell E. McCombs, "Mass Communication in Political Campaigns: Information, Gratification, and Persuasion." In F. Gerald Kline and Philip J. Tichenor (eds.), *Current Perspectives in Mass Communication Research* (Beverly Hills: Sage Publications, 1972), pp. 169–94.

[11]Walter DeVries and V. Lance Tarrance, Jr., *The Ticket-Splitter: A New Force in American Politics* (Grand Rapids: William B. Eerdmans Publishing Company, 1972).

*

8 The Impact of Issue Saliences

LEE B. BECKER
Ohio State University

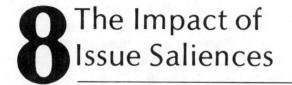

> ... the press's business is selling things and trying to enlighten and
> entertain people. You can only sell things that people are going to read.
> You can't force them to read.
>
> Garry Wills, "Picking a Winner"
> (episode of PBS television program *Behind the Lines*
> originally broadcast February 5, 1975)

When the political strategists attempt to formulate the issues of the campaign, they do so for the somewhat obvious reason that they think the issues will have some impact on the election outcome. Each strategist hopes the campaign will be played out over the issues that are most favorable to his or her candidate. By ignoring some issues and stressing others, and getting the media to do the same, the politician hopes to win.

Issues, of course, can affect a campaign in two ways. First, the position a candidate takes on the issue can lead to support from the voters. And second, the mere fact that a candidate is identified with a prominent issue can be important, particularly if the issue is a general one and solutions are vaguely formulated. In addition to the effects of issues on candidate choice, other, equally important, consequences are possible. Voters can become more interested in a campaign and its outcome as a result of issues, actually learn more about the issues, and become more active in the campaign. Finally, the issues may determine just who votes on election day. Candidates, of course, are interested in these indirect effects of issues as well as the more direct ones on candidate choice.

Some Issues in Charlotte

To examine these expectations about the direct and indirect effects of issue saliences, the key variables in agenda-setting research, a series of analyses were performed on the Charlotte data. The issues of Vietnam and drugs were selected for analysis because both were rated relatively important by the voters. But these two issues were not highly related in the voters' minds; in the paired-comparison tests they showed relatively low negative correlations on the salience measures. Some voters clearly thought both issues were important; others thought only one of the two was. Only Vietnam was a key media agenda item, however. The topic of drugs was not emphasized by any of the news media.

Voters were classified into three groups: those who, based on the four presidential elections before 1972, voted for mostly Democrats; those who voted as often for a Democrat as a Republican; and those who voted for mostly Republicans.[1] This partisan variable was created because of its expected role in the analysis to follow. Democrats thinking Vietnam to be an important issue were expected to be interested and active in the campaign; Republicans were expected to show the reverse pattern.

For the drug issue, the effects should be reversed, with Republicans showing more interest and activity at higher levels of salience and Democrats showing lower levels on these variables with increased salience of the issues. Independents should act like the Democrats for Vietnam and the Republicans for drugs, reflecting the strengths of the party candidates on those issues.

Correlations between individual saliences of the two test issues and various indicators of interest and activity show that Democratic voters who thought Vietnam highly salient were more likely, as expected, to be interested in the campaign and its outcome when interviewed in June than were Democrats thinking Vietnam not salient (see Table 8–1).

Contrary to expectation, however, the normal Republican voters showed the same tendency, while those without a clear partisan voting history showed weak relationships more like Republicans than Democrats. The expected drug issue effects

Table 8–1 Correlations Between Issue Saliences and Activation Variables

	Saliences					
	Vietnam			Drugs		
Voting history:	Dems.	Mixed	Reps.	Dems.	Mixed	Reps.
Campaign interest (June; n=102, 60, 152)	.18*	.12	.18	.09	.13	−.02
Interest in outcome (June; n=102, 60, 152)	.19*	.04	.17	−.00	.12	−.07
Knowledge level (Oct.; n=75, 32, 98)	.09	−.14	.07	−.18*	.15	.09
Campaign activity (Oct.; n=75, 32, 98)	.24*	−.29	−.23*	−.27*	.01	−.14
Turnout (Nov.; n=72, 35, 97)	.14	−.21	.09	−.12	.05	−.11

Note: *Salience paired-comparison measures are from the June wave for Campaign Interest and Interest in Outcome; for the other variables, the October paired-comparison salience measures are used.*
*p<.05, one-tailed test.

on these early campaign variables for partisan voters did not appear. Only voters without clear partisan voting histories showed relationships greater than .10. As expected, voters with mixed voting histories seem to be activated by the salience of the drug issue.

Level of Knowledge

Level of knowledge about the issue of Vietnam was not clearly related to the Vietnam saliences (see Table 8–1). Democratic voters who thought drug problems to be an important issue did show lower levels of knowledge about the issue, however, and those voters with a mixed voting history showed the predicted relationship for both issues (though the relationships do not reach traditional levels of statistical significance). The lack of strong relationships for the knowledge variable may reflect that the measures were not tied specifically to knowledge of how the issues were involved in the campaign. Breadth of knowledge across each of the areas, however, was measured.

The campaign activity variable in Table 8–1 shows relatively strong relationships for five of the six comparisons. Those Democratic voters who thought Vietnam important were more likely to do such things as canvas voters, contribute money to the campaign, or attend a political rally or speech than Democratic voters who thought Vietnam unimportant.

Republicans, as expected, showed just the opposite tendency, as did the voters with mixed voting histories. For these voters, Nixon apparently did not offer the alternatives sought, and they decided to sit out much of the election. Democrats who thought drugs important were likely to also avoid campaign activity, as was expected. But Republicans showed this same behavior pattern. Perhaps the Nixon decision not to stress this issue late in the campaign kept these voters from associating their candidate with the issue. Salience of the drug issue and campaign activity was unrelated for the mixed history voters.

Voter Turnout

Actual turnout on election day shows a pattern of relationships almost identical to that shown for general campaign activity (see Table 8–1). Democrats who thought Vietnam important were more likely to go to the polls than their counterparts not holding this issue salient. Conversely, Democrats thinking the drug issue salient were more likely to stay home. Voters with mixed voting histories seemed to be kept from the polls by the high salience of Vietnam, although the drug salience variable again had no effect. Vietnam salience did not hold its earlier effect for Republicans and was almost unrelated to turnout. Again there is a suggestion that Nixon was unable to adequately mobilize those voters traditionally voting Republican with high salience ratings for the drug issue.

To eliminate the effects of attitudes and educational level from the findings presented in Table 8–1, these two variables were entered as controls in Table 8–2. In general, these relationships remain relatively unchanged, indicating that the saliences themselves are having the effects. Two exceptions to this pattern did surface for the voters with mixed voting histories. When campaign activity and turnout were considered, drug salience showed strong relationships in the predicted direction. The attitudes of voters and their level of education seemed to cloud this relationship. In general, however, Table 8–2 follows closely the relationships shown in Table 8–1; fewer relationships are significant, however, due in part to a decrease in the degrees of freedom in the partial correlation test.

The relationships between saliences of the two issues and actual voter choice are shown in Table 8–3. Those voters with mixed voting histories are eliminated from these analyses because of their small number. As predicted, Democratic voters who thought Vietnam an important issue in October were more likely to prefer McGovern than Democrats who did not think Vietnam important. But contrary to prediction, high salience for the drug issue also led to a preference for McGovern in October. For the Republicans, no difference surfaces for the Viet-

Table 8–2 Correlations Between Issue Saliences and Activation Variables: Controlling for Education and Attitude

| | Saliences | | | | | |
| | Vietnam | | | Drugs | | |
Voting history:	Dems.	Mixed	Reps.	Dems.	Mixed	Reps.
Campaign interest (June; n=102, 60, 152)	.16	.12	.19	.07	.13	−.02
Interest in outcome (June; n=102, 60, 152)	.19	.03	.19	−.01	.10	−.07
Knowledge level (Oct.; n=75, 32, 98)	.03	−.05	.06	−.15	.23	.10
Campaign activity (Oct.; n=75, 32, 98)	.14	−.21	−.24*	−.21	.21	−.13
Turnout (Nov.; n=72, 35, 97)	.06	−.15	.07	−.13	.18	−.09

Note: *Salience paired-comparison measures are from the June wave for Campaign Interest and Interest in Outcome; for the other variables, the October paired-comparison salience measures are used. All entries are second-order partials.*
*$p<.05$, one-tailed test.

nam issue and only a slight tendency for high drug salience to lead to preference for Nixon is in evidence.

When the actual November vote is examined, however, all relationships are as expected. Those Democratic voters who thought the war important showed a slight preference for McGovern while those Democrats thinking drugs important showed a slight preference away from McGovern. For Republicans, high salience of the war issue seemed to result in a falling away from the party's candidate while high salience of drugs led to acceptance of Nixon. Although these relationships were in the predicted direction it should be noted that all are slight and only the difference between Republicans with high and low Vietnam salience is significant at traditional levels.

Table 8–3 Relationships Between Issue Saliences and Candidate Choice

		Saliences			
		Vietnam		*Drugs*	
		Low	High	Low	High
Percent choosing candidate consistent with voting history					
October	Democrats	44.9% (22)	58.6% (17)	40.0% (10)	53.9% (28)
	Republicans	90.6% (48)	90.7% (39)	87.5% (28)	90.8% (59)
November	Democrats	68.8% (22)	71.4% (15)	72.2% (13)	68.6% (24)
	Republicans	100.0% (47)	92.3% (36)	92.9% (26)	98.3% (56)

Note: *Numbers in parentheses indicate number of individual cases in that cell.*

We might note, however, that the effects of Vietnam seem to decrease for Democrats between the October and November waves. Perhaps the Nixon attempt to diffuse this issue showed some consequences, at least with this group of voters. The president, after all, has tremendous power to focus attention on any given issue . . . or to downplay it by ignoring it, Watergate aside.

Attitudes and Issues

The small number of subjects available for this analysis make a direct control for attitudes impossible. Separate analyses of the effects of these attitudinal variables, however, indicate they are no better predictors of vote outcome than the saliences. The generally low correlations between the attitudes and saliences and the findings from Table 8–2 suggest the control is not a crucial one for understanding the pattern of effects of the saliences.

The "Narcotizing" Function of the Press

The findings presented here raise anew an interesting question about media effects posed, originally, by Lazarsfeld and Merton.[2] Exposure to information from the media, these authors argued, may serve to "narcotize" rather than energize the audience members. Readers and viewers of the news media may come to substitute knowing about problems of the day for doing something about them, they suggested. Would we rather read or view than take action? If so, then the news can have a dysfunctional effect on us by insulating us from action.

The data presented here, at least for issue saliences, partially support such a conclusion for some voters. The issue saliences that many acquired from the media led to interest in the campaign and to a greater extent to campaign activity in some cases, but in others these saliences led to lower activity levels and turnout.

A more direct test of this narcotizing notion, however, is provided by an examination of the relationships between knowledge level and both campaign activity and turnout. Knowledge displayed a fair amount of independence of the saliences, despite the expectation that those individuals with high saliences for a given issue would be stimulated to learn more about the issue. Knowledge of the two issues, on the other hand, shows relatively strong relationships to public affairs media exposure during the campaign (+.27 for Vietnam and +.26 for drugs). Controlling for education level reduces these relationships only slightly (+.21 for both knowledge variables). There is more evidence, therefore, of a direct effect of the media on knowledge

Table 8–4 Correlations Between Knowledge Levels and Activation Variables

	Knowledge					
	Vietnam			*Drugs*		
Voting history:	Dems.	Mixed	Reps.	Dems.	Mixed	Reps.
Campaign activity (Oct.; n=77, 32, 99)	.18	.35*	.08	.22	.21	.04
Turnout (Nov.; n=68, 34, 97)	.20	.17	.05	.36*	.10	.19*

Note: *Knowledge was measured in the October wave.*
p<.05, two-tailed test.

than an indirect effect through the saliences formed by the media.

Data provided in Table 8–4 show no evidence in support of the narcotizing dysfunction arguments, no evidence that people substitute news exposure for political action. All correlations are positive, although many are slight and not statistically significant. The evidence from these analyses, however, suggests that knowledge leads to action—or that at least they are related. Data shown in Table 8–5, however, argue for caution in this interpretation. When education level of voters is controlled, the relationships between knowledge and action are reduced. What is more important, at least in the case of the relationship between drug knowledge and turnout for the voters with mixed partisan histories, is that the relationship between knowledge and action becomes negative. Two other correlations for the mixed voters also become negative, although neither is greater than .10. There seems to be some evidence here, however, that for the voters without clear partisan leanings, knowledge may be substituted for action, as expected from the narcotizing arguments of Lazarsfeld and Merton. But for the majority of voters, this does not seem to be the case.

Table 8–5 Correlations Between Knowledge Levels and Activation Variables: Controlling for Education

	Knowledge					
	Vietnam			*Drugs*		
Voting history:	Dems.	Mixed	Reps.	Dems.	Mixed	Reps.
Campaign activity (Oct.; n=77, 32, 99)	.06	.12	.06	.13	−.03	.00
Turnout (Nov.; n=68, 34, 97)	.16	−.09	−.03	.33*	−.22	.11

Note: *Knowledge was measured in the October wave. All entries are first-order partials.*
$*p<.05$, two-tailed test.

Consequences of Agenda-Setting

The importance of agenda-setting as an area of research is enhanced to the extent consequences of issue salience formation can be demonstrated. The evidence for such effects is somewhat mixed here, but some patterns do seem to have emerged. Democrats seem to have been activated by the Vietnam issue. Republicans, too, were less likely to participate in the campaign activity if they thought Vietnam an important issue, but the war had little impact on turnout for this group. Democrats became less active if they thought drug problems were an important issue. In addition, the saliences seem to have direct effects on candidate choice: Democratic voters who thought the Vietnam war important seemed to be more likely to vote for McGovern while Republicans thinking drugs important were more likely to vote for Nixon.

While these findings are tentative because of the small number of cases involved and the lack of statistical significance in many cases, they do support the general expectations about the role of issue saliences in elections. Candidates seek to control issue saliences to better their chances of success, and these data suggest this is successful politics.

The data presented here show very limited evidence that knowledge of issues learned by voters from press exposure serves to "narcotize" voters and keep them from the polls. Only voters without clear patterns of partisan voting showed any (weak) tendency to substitute news reading or viewing for political action, although for some types of voters there was an association between certain issues (here we focused on Vietnam and drugs) and different levels of political activity. To a limited extent, issues can send us to the polls or keep us away.

NOTES

[1] Voters were classified on the basis of the number of elections out of the four possible they actually voted in. First time voters, therefore, were eliminated from these analyses as well as those who voted for Wallace in 1968. For other voters, a Wallace vote in 1968 was counted as a non-partisan vote since Wallace ran as an independent that year.

[2] Paul F. Lazarsfeld and Robert K. Merton, "Mass Communication, Popular Taste and Organized Social Action," in Lyman Bryson (ed.), The Communication of Ideas (New York: Institute for Religious and Social Studies, 1948), pp. 95–118.

*

9 Agenda-Setting and the Young Voter

L. EDWARD MULLINS
University of Alabama

> *Pollytics and bankin' is the on'y two games where age has th' best iv it. Youth has betther things to attind to, an' more iv thim.*

Finley Peter Dunne, *Observations*

What is most characteristic of young Americans? A rock in the hand or hand on the voting lever? Are young voters likely to adapt to the established political system or attempt to change it, and what role is played in their lives by the mass media?

The 1972 presidential election was potentially the first national election for more than 25,000,000 new voters between the ages of 18 and 24. This election, coming after a decade of sometimes violent youthful political activism which concluded with massive student strikes and anti-war demonstrations in the spring of 1970, was especially important because of passage of the 26th Amendment lowering the legal voting age from 21 to 18.

How well did these newly enfranchised young voters meet this new responsibility? And, how much were these young voters influenced by the political news agenda of the news media? These are the questions of importance in this chapter.

The Participation
of the Young Voter

Viewed as a short-range civics lesson, their participation in the 1972 election was disappointing. Their turnout, under 40 percent, was the lowest of any age group in an election that saw about 60 percent of the eligible voters go to the polls. But turnout, although important, is only one measure of involvement.

Interest in and learning about politics results from a developmental process, and therefore the youthful participation in the 1972 presidential election may be viewed profitably as an important early lesson with implications for future political socialization. Interest among young people, both on and off the campus, ran high in the 1972 election.

The concomitants of that interest will be explored here, using data from the Charlotte study plus a comparative study done on the University of North Carolina campus at Chapel Hill.[1]

Much of what is learned from the mass media results from a process of incidental learning. That is, learning from the mass media may be thought of as any modification of behavior or cognition as a result of practice, whether explicitly intended by the source or receiver or not. Such a learning orientation suggests several basic hypotheses regarding the process of agenda-setting:

1. The greater the complexity of cognitive structures (located crudely by level of education) the more likely will young voters learn campaign issues from the mass media. In other words, those with more educational experience will be

more competent to learn those issues. We have called this the "competence" hypothesis.

2. Media agenda-setting among young voters will vary directly with the level of general exposure to the media and to messages about the issues in particular. In other words, the greater the exposure, the greater the learning. We have called this the "individual practice" hypothesis.

3. Agenda-setting among young voters varies directly with amount of interpersonal communication about political issues. Put simply: the more you talk *and listen* to your family and friends, the more likely you are to learn about issues (from people who very often themselves have learned about them from the news media). We have called this the "social practice" hypothesis.

4. Because of the fewer number of issues carried by the medium, television will influence the saliency of relatively fewer issues than do newspapers. Conversely, daily newspapers, which have more room to cover more issues, influence the salience of a greater number of issues.

Young Voter Issues

In Chapel Hill young voters were asked: "Regardless of what the candidates are saying, what two or three issues do you think are the most important in the 1972 election?" In Charlotte, young voter agendas were constructed from two questions: "First, what are you most concerned about these days?" and "What about national problems? Which of them are you most concerned about?"

For young voters in 1972, whether college exposed or not, the Vietnam War was the most important issue. This is not surprising. The war and the peace negotiations to end it were number one in the minds of a majority of all Americans. Twenty-eight

percent of the Chapel Hill voters and 31 percent of young Charlotte voters cited the war as an issue. For both, next came the
issue of the economy/inflation/cost of living.

College versus
Noncollege Voters

But beyond the war and rising cost of living the two groups of
young voters largely disagreed on their rankings of important
political issues. Some differences no doubt result from the variation in the wording of a question, but the differences (see
Table 9-1) also seem to reflect a range of psychological en-
vironments. In a sense, college students were more altruistic
and idealistic, whereas noncollege youth were more likely to
interpret political issues according to their own self interest.

After the war and economy, the three issues mentioned most
frequently by the college students suggest a concern for an extended social environment. These issues—human rights and
welfare, the environment, and international problems—are not
as egocentric as the comparably ranked issues of the young
Charlotte voters. The issues of these young voters—a vague uncertainty about the election itself, crime/drugs, and personal
education problems (mainly a desire for better educa-
tion/training)—suggest that these young, mostly working-
class, voters tend to define national problems in terms of their
own world. For them political issues are not so abstract; they
leave that to their college-exposed brethren.

Number of Issues Cited

Other striking differences in the issue agendas of the two
groups are the absence of any mention of Watergate or government scandal by the noncollege voters and the relatively high

Table 9–1 How Young Voters Rated The Issues

College Youth

Issue	Percentage of Total Issues Mentioned	Rank
Vietnam war	28%	1
Inflation/economy	16	2
Human rights and welfare	15	3
Environment/ecology	13	4
International problems	12	5
Gov't scandal/watergate	9	6
Crime/violence	4	7
Pupil busing	2%	8
	99%	

(No. of issues mentioned =737)
(No. of students=292)

Non-College Youth

Issue	Percentage of Total Issues Mentioned	Rank
Vietnam war	31%	1
Inflation/economy	18	2
The election	16	3
Crime/drugs	8	4
Education problems	8	4
Environment/ecology	6	6
Personal worries/family	6	6
Human rights and welfare	6%	6
	99%	

(No. of issues mentioned=60)

(No. of youth=54)

(Failure to total 100 percent due to rounding)
(Multiple answers permitted)

ranking of crime/drugs and low ranking of environmental issues by the noncollege voters. In addition, the college voters
voiced more issue concerns, an average of 2.5 each compared
to 1.1 for the noncollege voters. More educated young voters
expressed awareness of a wider, and less purely personal,
world of political issues and concerns.

While more interested in the issue of governmental honesty
than their noncollege counterparts, the young Chapel Hill
voters (like the rest of the nation) were slow to raise the Watergate corruption issue to a top spot. Apparently for most of them
the issue did not particularly affect their issue perceptions
during the election. A year later, after televised Senate hear-
ings on the Watergate scandals, the issue of governmental
honesty had become the hottest issue on the campus, and was
near the top nationally.[2]

Young Voter Agendas
and Media Agendas

Media agendas, determined by monitoring network early
evening news programs and content analysis of newspapers,
appear in Table 9–2. The agendas of the four media are moderately to highly intercorrelated. Correlations range from .38
to .90.

Because several issues highlighted by the media were not
mentioned by the young Charlotte voters, technically it is not
possible to test the hypothesis that media agendas influence issue saliences for all issues. The question becomes what influence the media had on the issues which were mentioned; what
is the fit between emphasis by the media and emphasis by
young voters? Therefore if we exclude from both media and
voter agendas the issues which did not appear for both groups,
we can make rough comparisons between the two groups for
media agenda-setting effects.

Table 9-2 Media Issue Agendas[1]/Correlations

Issue	Raleigh News & Observer	Charlotte Observer	NBC News	CBS News
Vietnam war	1	1	1	2
Economy/inflation	2	3	3	3
Human rights/welfare	3	2	7	4
Government scandal	4	4	2	1
Environment/ecology	5	6	5	6
International relations	6	7	4	7
Crime/violence	7	5	8	5
Busing	8	8	6	8

	N&O	Observer	NBC	CBS
N&O	—	.90	.64	.79
Observer		—	.38	.83
NBC			—	.60
CBS				—

(Correlations are Spearman r)

[1]*Relative newspaper agendas were established by tabulating the column inches, excluding headlines. TV agendas resulted from adding up seconds devoted to each "issue" story. The periods compared differ somewhat from those reflected in Chapter 3, hence the rankings differ somewhat.*

Table 9-3 provides pertinent data. The upper half of the table contains the Charlotte group's agenda and the agendas of NBC Nightly News, CBS Evening News (the two networks most seen by both sets of young voters who are compared here), and the Charlotte *Observer* and Raleigh *News and Observer*. Voter and media issues not common to both groups are not included.

The middle section of the table contains the agendas cited by college youth compared with the media agendas while the lower section of the table shows pertinent Spearman's Rho correlations.

Table 9-3 Agenda-Setting Among Campus and Non-Campus Youth

Issue	Non-College Rank	NBC	CBS	Charlotte Observer
Vietnam war	1	1	1	1
Economy/inflation	2	2	2	3
Crime/drugs	3	5	4	4
Environment/ecology	4	3	5	5
Human rights/welfare	4	4	3	2

Issue	College group Rank	NBC	CBS	Raleigh News & Observer
Vietnam war	1	1	2	1
Economy/inflation	2	3	3	2
Human rights/welfare	3	7	4	3
Environment/ecology	4	5	6	5
International relations	5	4	7	6
Government scandal	6	2	1	4
Crime/violence	7	8	5	7
Busing	8	6	8	8

Agenda-Setting Correlations

	Non-College	College Group	Differences (NC–C)
NBC	.75	.52	+.23
CBS	.85	.52	+.33
Charlotte Observer	.65 Raleigh News & Observer	.93	−.28

The "Competence" Hypothesis

Both groups of young voters tended to hold issue saliences which were moderately to highly intercorrelated with media emphasis. Yet if we take level of formal education as a rough locator of cognitive complexity, we do find evidence that the greater the cognitive complexity, the greater the learning of issues from newspapers, but not television news.

By contrast, we find that less formally educated voters were much more likely to go along with the issue emphasis of the television evening news. The differences column at the bottom of the table shows how television news asserted its power over the political agendas of the less formally educated Charlotte voters while the reverse pattern held true for newspapers.

Influence of Frequency
of Media Exposure

One principle of learning is that frequent stimuli are more influential than less frequent stimuli on learning. Put simply: the more young voters see or read the news, the more likely they will tend to absorb media issues as their own. We have called this the "individual practice" hypothesis.

To test this hypothesis we assumed that level of exposure is a form of learning practice, and controlled for it in the analysis. The results appear in Table 9-4.

As newspaper exposure increases from low (read the paper once or twice a week) to high (read the paper everyday or nearly every day), the correlations increase from .86 to .98. But for television, correlations increase from low to intermediate exposure, but then decline or remain the same.

This finding suggests that an information versus pleasure-seeking characteristic of our voter viewers may have affected results. Student users of the newspaper, for example, were

Table 9-4 Media/Student Agenda Correlations By Level of Media Exposure

Newspaper Exposure	N&O	Television Exposure	CBS	NBC
Low (N=74)	.86	Low (N=112)	.47	.41
Medium (N=67)	.88	Medium (N=74)	.62	.62
High (N=150)	.98	High (N=106)	.42	.62

most likely to use the newspaper for news and public affairs, while television was more often used for entertainment and diversion.

Perhaps the reason for similar correlations at the highest as well as moderate levels of television exposure is that voters were seeking pleasure and therefore only incidentally absorbed any political information coming along. A recent political study in England has suggested that simply liking to watch television, aside from any pleasure in viewing political news, can be an important variable in explaining how even voters with low political motivations learn about some issues.[3] Voters cannot escape, at least without changing their media behavior. Turning off the tube is far easier to suggest than to do.

We attempted to control for interest in news by dividing the young Chapel Hill voters into groups claiming to have high or low interest in newspaper or television news. This manipulation partially supported the hypothesis that an interest in the news on a given medium increases the likelihood that a voter will reflect that medium's issue emphasis.

For example, young student voters who professed keen interest in television news reflected the CBS news issue emphasis closely (+.90), while those with less news interest rated the issues less like CBS (+.62). The same was true for the newspaper. For NBC, however, differences were in the opposite direction. This may be explained by the fact that the CBS Evening News program was preferred by nearly a three to one margin over NBC nightly News. Those NBC programs most mentioned

Table 9-5 Agenda-Setting by Amount of News Interest, Interpersonal Communication, and Group Memberships for Students

News Interest		N&O	CBS	NBC
Low news interest (Newspaper=91) (TV=146)		.78	.62	.75
High news interest (Newspaper =201) (TV=146)		.92	.90	.65
Interpersonal communication	Low	.88	.48	.50
	High	.98	.67	.57
Belonging to groups	Low	.98	.67	.57
	High	.71	.31	.38

by the young college voters were entertainment, not news, programs. Taken as a whole, these data provide support for what we have called the individual practice hypothesis.

Young Voters and Interpersonal Communications

The press, of course, is not the only political information source. We live amid a virtual sea of voices, some as demanding of our attention as a fog horn, others as subtle as the tide changing. Among these, interpersonal communication—talk with family and friends—is an important source of political information and opinion. We were able to test effects of interpersonal communication among the young college voters.

Discussion of politics is nearly universal during an election,
even among people who ordinarily are not attentive to public
affairs. Within a learning context, we can think of interpersonal communication as providing an opportunity for group
practice (reception and sending) of political messages. Our
"social practice" hypothesis argues that the more frequent
this interpersonal discussion about campaign issues, the
higher the level of agenda-setting.

Although some have argued that interpersonal communication could just as easily lead to blocking as to facilitating
agenda-setting, our hypothesis argues that discussion of campaign issues provides another opportunity for young voters to
pick up issues first spread by the mass media. The bull session
is a well known and usually fondly remembered feature of college life. One should also point out, however, that it may be that
many young voters who engage a great deal in interpersonal
communication anticipate a need for fresh information in order
to appear informed—or simply to be able to keep up the chatter—and therefore more readily attend to the media. Which-
ever way this works, if in fact it does not work both ways, in
this study there was an association between level of interpersonal communication and level of agenda-setting. Table 9–5
(middle two rows) supports our social practices hypothesis in
every instance.

Another comparison, however, does provide support for the
blocking hypothesis of group influence (lower two rows). We
divided student voters into those who belonged to organizations
actively working on behalf of a campaign organization and
those who did not. Issue emphases of those belonging to these
groups were less like those of the news media than were those
who did not belong to such groups. Perhaps these organizations
themselves raise issues which compete with those of the media.
After all, many if not most political organizations are organized
around particular issues. Their very function is to thrust certain issues high up the agenda, first with their own members
and then voters at large.

By contrast, the young voters who lacked the anchor of a
group-generated agenda were more likely to reflect the issue

emphasis of the news media. These voters have less competition in deciding on their own important issues. Looking at Table 9-5, one is led to conclude that young college-exposed voters will be more susceptible to the media agenda (social practices hypothesis) if they engaged more heavily in interpersonal communication, but less if they belong to political groups. The same comparisons could not be made for the Charlotte young voters. Clearly more work is needed in this area. Surely it is not as simple as bull session versus political group membership.

The Influence of Television's "Big" Evening News Story

The final hypothesis, that television agenda-setting is more influential with regard to the single most salient issue rating by young voters, is given support by dividing the agendas suggested by the college-exposed young voters into three groups: those issues mentioned *first* by these voters; the first two mentioned added together to form a single ranking; and *all* issues mentioned (average number mentioned was 2.5) added together to form a single issue ranking. Presumably the issue mentioned first is most salient to the individual young voter. Young Charlotte voters individually mentioned too few issues to make this same comparison possible.

The newspaper voter issue comparisons tended to become stronger as second and third mentions were added, but as hypothesized, the television news/voter agendas declined in strength with the same comparisons (see Table 9-6). It therefore appears that the impact of television political news is different, more powerful and immediate, than the impact of the more extensive but less dramatic newspaper political news coverage. Here young voters appear similar to voters in general.

Thus it seems that television's emphasis on one or two issues at any given time had an effect on the single most important is-

Table 9–6 Inter-media Issue Ranking Correlations

Newspaper	N&O	Observ.
Most important issue	.79	.62
First two issues	.91	.79
First three issues	.93	.79
Networks	NBC	CBS
Most important issue	.71	.61
First two issues	.55	.60
First three issues	.52	.43

sue which the young voters held important, while newspapers affected the recollection of a greater number of issues.

The television and newspaper news coverage patterns also help explain this difference. For example, the top two issues on CBS (Watergate and the Vietnam War) accounted for nearly 70 percent of its news emphasis during the period the news was content analyzed for this analysis, while the Raleigh *News and Observer* and Charlotte *Observer* devoted only 45 percent of their news coverage to these topics during the same period. Television far more than newspapers focuses on major news topics.

Television appeared to function as a sort of front page for our college-exposed young voters while newspapers appeared to help these young voters recall issues which had been on the political agenda over a period of time.

Similarities Across
Age Groups

This analysis of how issues were learned in the 1972 presidential election by a group of college and noncollege young voters getting their first chance to vote for President supports the view that media agenda-setting does occur for political issues. This learning often appears incidental to their media use habits or group affiliations, the same as for older voters.

Although they tended to hold to somewhat different issues as important, both college and noncollege groups absorbed at least some of the issues emphasized by the news media. As has been true with many other studies,[4] newspapers were more influential with those of higher formal education while television was the leader with those of lesser education.

Regardless of educational level, young voters with greater news interest recalled more issues than did those without this interest. Similarly, simple exposure to a news medium, especially newspapers, was likely to lead to more learning of the news agenda. For television, this finding is not as strong. Young voters were similar to voters of all ages. Apparently there is no great generation gap here between young and older voters. Whatever political world our young may plan to create, they necessarily begin by focusing on the same one we all do.

NOTES

[1]L. E. Mullins, "Mass Communication on the Campus: A Descriptive and Causal Analysis of Information-Seeking and Political Behavior During the 1972 Presidential Election," Unpublished Ph.D. dissertation, University of North Carolina at Chapel Hill, 1974.

Data on political issues regarded as important as well as media most used for political news were gathered from a systematic random sample of 292 full time UNC undergraduates in late October 1972. For comparison purposes, issues and media questions were similar to those used in the larger Charlotte study. The Charlotte study had 54 young voters who were not college educated. Therefore this chapter examines the influence of the media agenda on young voters and, where possible, compares the college-associated voters in Chapel Hill with young voters without a college education in Charlotte.

In addition to the media content analyzed for the Charlotte study (Charlotte *Observer* and ABC, NBC, and CBS evening news), the Chapel Hill study content-analyzed the pertinent political news from the Raleigh *News and Observer*, a newspaper heavily read by students. The content analysis categories were substantially the same for both studies. The content analysis data cited in the Chapel Hill study, however, refer only to October 15–21, 1972 the week just before the students in Chapel Hill were interviewed.

[2]See *Gallup Opinion Digest*, March, 1973, p. 11.

[3]Jay G. Blumler and Denis McQuail, *Television in Politics: Its Uses and Influence* (Chicago: University of Chicago Press, 1969).

[4]See the research volumes, *News Research for Better Newspapers* (New York: ANPA Foundation).

10 Agenda-Setting and the Political Process

MAXWELL E. McCOMBS
Syracuse University

DONALD L. SHAW
University of North Carolina at Chapel Hill

> *More thorough and widespread knowledge of the basic process of converting demands into agenda items can contribute to making the political system more effective and responsive.*
>
> Cobb and Elder, *Participation in American Politics: The Dynamics of Agenda-Building.* 1972, p. 170.

Mass communication is a major item on our contemporary cultural agenda. Considerable popular and scholarly commentary focuses on a wide variety of media effects. How televised violence has affected our children, whether advertising has turned America into a hedonistic consumer society, how the vast amounts of time spent with newspapers, magazines, and television eliminate other possible uses of our leisure time—these are a few of the critical social questions about the effects of mass communication. While these questions about communication effects are often framed in pejorative terms, there exists another set of parallel questions on communication effects that are framed in highly optimistic, if not laudatory, terms. These questions focus on the ability of mass communication to extend our cognitive worlds, to bring us new experiences and information, to continue the education process beyond the formal boundaries of the high school and college classroom. In short, mass communication effects can be bad or good.

While there has been scholarly concern over both kinds of effects for more than a quarter of a century, only recently have we turned to a more precise study of how the mass communication influence process actually operates. A major attraction of the concept of agenda-setting as a perspective for probing this influence process has been that agenda-setting brings together in a single concept both audience behavior and mass media content, discrete elements which in the past have been treated separately.

A political campaign is a key place to study mass communication influence because media behavior is intimately connected with how our political environment is perceived, how our agenda of public issues is shaped, and how we cast our votes. In other words, the political agenda of the mass media is highly related to the shape of political power.

Beyond the specific behaviors of an election, it also is important to understand how competing groups in our society influence the shape of the political issues which concern all of us (and sometimes are critical in the outcome of a particular election). Every society must have processes by which the myriad problems, concerns, and questions of its many citizens are translated into succinct issues, are operationalized in government action of some sort, and perhaps finally are perpetuated as cultural values.

In a society as large as the United States, if a group does not have access to an interested mass medium—either through the intrinsic appeal of its special interest or through the availability of extensive financial resources—we simply will never learn of its concern. Or, as was the case with Vietnam and civil rights, concerned groups will have to take to the streets to convert their concern into an event that the news media ultimately will translate as an issue. Unfortunately, the news media are more attentive to new events than to new ideas. So the study of the agenda-setting process is crucial to our attempts to achieve a better interchange of ideas and a smoother process of social change within our society.

The Press's Contribution

The Fourth Estate's contribution to the agenda-setting process of our society is implied in that very label for the press. As a Fourth Estate, the press is an independent force whose dialogue with the other elements of society produces the agenda of issues considered by political elites and voters. The press is far more than a conduit for the concerns and issues of others. In the process of transmitting others' concerns and issues, it reworks and retranslates them. In the process of deciding each day which items to report and which to ignore, the editors of the news media guide our attention to elements in the larger political arena. They not only guide and direct, they actually supply the building blocks we use in constructing our mental mosaics of the political arena. The mass media both focus attention and structure our cognitions.

This means that the mass media are the major artisans of our popular political culture, of what the masses of voters perceive to be political reality and the political concerns of the day. It also means that the mass media are major shapers of our elite political culture. Witness the major role of the elite press as a source of information among major decision-makers. Through its winnowing of the day's happenings to find the major events, concerns, and issues, the press inadvertently plays an agenda-setting influence role. While this influence role of the press may be considered a negative effect by some, it clearly has a positive side. Both by deliberate winnowing and by inadvertent agenda-setting the mass media help society achieve consensus on which concerns and interests should be translated into public issues and opinion.

The Role of
the Audience

While the mass media play a key role in the translation process that yields the public issues of the day, they are not the exclusive determiners of the public agenda. There is an interplay between the press and its sources that affects the press agenda, and most importantly, there is interaction between the press and the public that affects what is *accepted* as the public agenda. In the concept of agenda-setting may lie the organizing, explanatory principle for many of the discrete findings of the past about audience behavior, the process of mass communication, and the social effects of mass communication.

This concept becomes particularly exciting as a bridge between the macro and micro approaches to mass communication analysis. The idea of an agenda-setting function of the press is a macro-notion of mass communication influence. But the movement toward a real theory of agenda-setting has advanced the farthest in its definition of the micro-variables which specify the contingent conditions for this agenda-setting influence to appear among individual citizens. Since mass communication is a vertical discipline pursuing a substantive interest across numerous levels of analysis—in contrast to horizontal disciplines such as psychology and sociology which pursue a variety of substantive interests across a single level of analysis—concepts which bridge these levels of analysis have high value.

The new empirical findings reported in this volume have buttressed two parts of this bridge. At the macro-level, additional evidence (including the first unambiguous causal evidence) of an agenda-setting function of the press has been documented.

At the micro-level, important new evidence has been presented about the link between the agenda-setting influence of the press and frequency of exposure to mass communication, individual levels of need for orientation, and frequency of interpersonal communication. This evidence yields a more precise description of what we mean by agenda-setting.

Frequency of Mass Media Exposure

Agenda-setting influence among individuals is directly related to their frequency of exposure to mass communication. This is the first theoretical statement added to the original assertion of an agenda-setting function of the press. Over a dozen analyses relevant to this question have been reported. Some examined agenda-setting among students, others adult voters in Charlotte during the 1972 presidential campaign; some used cross-sectional data and some used the across-time data available from the panel; some focused on the agenda-setting influence of television while others examined newspaper influence. The preponderance of the evidence shows higher levels of agreement between personal agendas and mass media agendas among those individuals most frequently exposed to mass communication. An additional finding from the 1972 Charlotte voter study underscores the major agenda-setting potential of the mass media and the importance of the exposure hypothesis. There is a progressive increase in the use of mass communications during the presidential campaign. In fact, the major political role of the mass media may be to raise the salience of politics among the American electorate every four years. Once politics has become salient and voters make increasingly frequent use of the mass media to monitor the campaign, the stage is set for the agenda-setting influence of the press.

Paralleling the increased use of mass communication during the course of the presidential campaign is an increase in the number of political conversations among voters. As television and newspapers make politics more salient to the voters, they also express a growing need for information about the candidates and issues. This sense of information-need leads to increased use of both interpersonal and mass communication. What is the outcome of all this in terms of agenda-setting? There is some evidence that daily discussants of politics and especially those who assume an advocacy role in this discussion best reflect the mass media's agenda of issues. Rather than competing with the mass communication agenda, interpersonal communication appears to reinforce this agenda. Only where an issue is especially salient to an individual—as among members of special interest groups—is interpersonal communication likely to block the agenda-setting influence of the press.

Another way of expressing this need for information in psychological terms is to describe an individual's need for orientation in the political arena. Analyses focusing on the role of need for orientation in media use and in agenda-setting show both strong links between need for orientation and use of the mass media to follow politics, and (in line with the "frequency of exposure" hypothesis) strong links between need for orientation and reflection of the mass media's agenda of public issues. While the correlations between individual agendas and newspaper agendas increase directly with the level of need for orientation, the relationship with television agendas is much weaker. This is one hint of a significant difference in the agenda-setting roles of newspapers and television. But before pursuing that point, it is important to note that these findings on the mediating role in the agenda-setting process of need for orientation and of need for information serve to link the long dominant effects orientation of mass communication research with the uses-and-gratifications approach to the study of mass communication.

Newspapers and Television

Newspapers and television play distinct agenda-setting roles. In Charlotte during 1972 the newspaper showed a stronger initial match with voters' issue concerns in June than did the two TV networks. And, over the summer and early fall, the newspaper agenda influenced the voter concerns expressed in October. Despite these early advantages for the newspaper in wielding agenda-setting influence, by October voter concerns showed a better match with the current TV agenda than with the current newspaper agenda of October.

Was it a matter of "TV catching up" with the newspaper and the public? For the newspapers the available evidence clearly says "No". There is no evidence for any agenda-setting within the media or any two-step flow of issue salience from the newspaper to television. For the public, the answer is—at least partially—"Yes." There is public influence on the TV agenda across time. By October the TV networks were better attuned to their audience's agenda, more so in fact than was the newspaper. These increased levels of agreement might result simply from feedback, but the superiority of the TV match also suggests some agenda-setting influence by television in the final weeks of the campaign.

To sum up, there are two distinct phases in election year agenda-setting. In the summer and early fall the prime mover is the newspaper alone. Newspapers perform more of an initiating role in public opinion than does television. With their greater channel capacity—dozens and dozens of pages in contrast to a half hour for most TV news presentations—newspapers can pick issues at an earlier point in their life cycle. But as we move into the fall campaign period, this influence of the press built up across time is shared with television. Since there are major stylistic as well as technological dissimilarities between newspapers and television, this later phase in agenda-setting is sharing rather than reinforcement.

There also is a major demographic difference in the typical public affairs audience of the two news media which accents their different roles in the agenda-setting process. This difference is underlined by the finding that voters with a high level of education showed greater agreement with the newspaper's agenda while voters with lower levels of education showed greater agreement with the television agenda of public issues. The differential effects of the two media also depend on the nature of the personal agenda. Newspapers have more influence on the intra-personal agenda of issues, those issues considered personally most important, while television has more influence on inter-personal agendas, what people talk about with each other. This is compatible with the earlier evidence that newspapers wield long-term influence while television fills a short-term influence role.

The nature of the agenda-setting role also may differ for the two media. There is some evidence that television agenda-setting is best described as matching saliences—general agreement on what the top stories of the day are—while newspaper agenda-setting is best described by the more radical notion of matching specific priorities—the rank ordering of issues suggested by the newspaper becomes the rank ordering of individuals' issue priorities. Both are instances of significant social effects where issues are placed at the top of the public agenda by the mass media.

Appendix: Using Polls and Content Analysis to Study an Election

MARY ELIZABETH JUNCK
Miami *Herald* Publishing Company, Miami

MAXWELL E. McCOMBS
Syracuse University

DONALD L. SHAW
University of North Carolina at Chapel Hill

> We are filters. It is through our smudgy, hand-held prisms that the voters meet the candidates and grow to love them or hate them, trust them or distrust them. We are the voters' eyes and ears, and we are more than that, for, sometimes we perform a larger and, some would say, a more controversial function. We write the rules and we call the game.
>
> James Perry, Us & Them:
> How the Press Covered the 1972 Election

During the 1972 national election the research team represented in this book used surveys and content analysis to pursue an integrated view of mass communication and voter behavior in Charlotte, North Carolina, a metropolitan area with a third of a million people located about halfway between Washington, D.C., and Atlanta, Georgia. Since the initial empirical probe of agenda-setting had been conducted only four years earlier during the 1968 presidential election,[1] this is the first major push forward to explicate empirically the concept of agenda-setting.

Data on voters came from a sample survey. Since the concept of agenda-setting clearly asserts a cause-and-effect relationship across time between media content and voters' thoughts about the election, our interviews with the voters were designed as a panel survey in which randomly selected voters were interviewed at three different times during the 1972 campaign. By interviewing the same persons at three moments in time, clear data on the time-order of changes in voters' thoughts—data which can be compared to the shifts over time in media content—are available for causal analysis.

When voters are interviewed at only one point in time, correlations between their responses and the media content can be established, but not the *direction of effect*. With panel data on the voters and chronological data on media content, this chicken-and-egg problem of which came first is eliminated.

This survey portion of the Charlotte study began in June 1972. The Mecklenburg County (North Carolina) Board of Elections provided a random sample from the more than 150,000 names on the county voter rolls. The sample was produced by computer from a master tape containing the entire roster of county voters.

Interviewing began on June 10 and ended on June 30, yielding 380 usable interviews. Interviewing was cut off on June 30 because of the July 4 holiday weekend and the approaching Democratic convention opening in Miami on July 10.

Thirty-five interviewers were used for the June wave of the survey, most of them residents of the Charlotte area. Eleven of the interviewers were students out of school for the summer; many others were housewives. There were three school teachers and one social worker. Most of the interviewers were in their early 20s, and 23 of them were women. A number had worked on other survey projects in the Charlotte area.

The 380 interviews obtained are not necessarily a microcosm of the Mecklenburg County voter registration rolls. Nor need they be since the county election board estimates that between twelve and twenty percent of the names listed for each precinct are invalid because those people have died or moved away. Thus the characteristics of the total population of registered voters need not match our sample because the universe of names on the registration rolls is actually a pseudouniverse. It may or may not correspond in such characteristics as age and sex to the "real" population of eligible Charlotte and Mecklenburg County voters in the 1972 presidential election.

This lack of correspondence is the major reason for an imperfect match between the Charlotte sample and the total registration. Refusals to be interviewed is another, although negligible, source for any lack of fit. Only a few scattered respondents contacted by an interviewer refused to be interviewed. A somewhat more significant factor is absence from home during the interviewing period. Obviously, some people were vacationing during the June survey period. Others happened to be away from home when the interviewer called. Some were never contacted even when the interviewer made three or more callbacks.

Any comparison of the sample used here with the actual population of registered voters must be made, then, with these three factors in mind—voters whose names have not yet been purged from the rolls, refusals, and not-at-homes.

Finally, it should be emphasized that our purpose in June—and also in October and November—was *not* to describe the opinions or behavior of Charlotte voters nor to estimate voter characteristics. A perfectly representative sample is requisite for such goals. Rather the goal of the Charlotte study was to match voter attributes from the survey with media attributes from the content analysis. The major requirement for such a comparison is sufficient variation in each set of data to test the relationships asserted by the idea of an agenda-setting function of the press. The exact distribution of this variance among the sample, however, need not match the distribution among the total population.

Given this goal and the inexactness of any voter registration roll in comparison with the population in general, the most important comparisons are internal to the panel of voters themselves. Obviously, everyone interviewed in the first wave will not be available for a second and third interview later in the campaign. Some people move away, a few die, and a few refuse to be interviewed a second or third time. While 380 voters were successfully interviewed during June 1972 in Charlotte, a sizable number of these people moved away from Charlotte before our second wave of interviewing began in mid-October. This transient character of a significant portion of the Charlotte population is noted in our description of the city.

During late October 230 voters originally interviewed in June were successfully reinterviewed. Also, because only a small number of Black voters were available for analysis, 41 additional Black voters were added to the panel in October. Both the June and October interviews were face-to-face contacts with the voters. The same interviewers used in June were used again in October.

The third wave of interviews was conducted by telephone in November during the ten days immediately following the national election. Since little time intervened between the October and November interviews, attrition from the panel was minimal. Out of the 271 October interviews (230 repeats from June plus 41 new interviews with Blacks), 254 were successfully reinterviewed in November by graduate students from the University of North Carolina.

Table A–1 sums up the various groups of voters resulting from these three interviews. The largest group was the panel of 227 voters interviewed all three times during the campaign. The second largest group (147 voters) was composed of those voters who were interviewed only in June. Follow-up checks on these voters revealed that the vast majority had moved away from North Carolina. The basic analysis for this 1972 study of the role of mass communication in a political campaign was based on the 227 members of the three-wave panel plus the 24 Blacks added in October and successfully reinterviewed in November. Focusing on change over time, several chapter analyses used only the panel of 227.

Table A–1

Dates of interviews	June	October	November
*June/October/November	227	227	227
June only	147	X	X
June/October only	3	3	X
June/November only	3	X	3
*New Black voters (June/October/November)	(24)	24	24
New Black voters (June/October only)	(17)	17	X
TOTALS:	421	271	254

*Note: When the 41 new Black voters were added to the panel in October, they also were asked all the "fixed" items from the June interview; for example, their level of education and annual income. Thus, their files contain complete data for both June and October questions except for items specifically included to measure change between these two times, such as the issue which each voter considered most important at each point during the campaign.

Before looking at these various analyses, it was important to make an internal comparison of the voters in each "wave," or series, of interviewing. Any changes found in the variables of paramount interest, such as voters' perceptions of what were the key issues, could possibly have resulted from shifts in the composition of the panel itself, not from mass communication inputs. A key assumption in using the panel was that attrition

from the panel was random. It was assumed that attrition did
not occur disproportionately among any particular type of person and cause apparent changes in the variables of key interest, changes that really were due to changes in the composition
of the panel itself.

The best way to check this assumption of random attrition
from the panel was to examine demographic variables, which
should not change over time. The demographics considered
here were race, sex, political party, age, education, and income.

The Charlotte sample was quite constant during each of the
three series of interviews (see Table A–2). The differences
among waves were minor. None of them exceeded the sample
error, set quite stringently at 4.9 percent. In fact, only one demographic variable was greater than 4 percent. It seems safe to
conclude that there was no cause for suspecting that the
"kinds" of people in the sample, at least in terms of the six
demographic variables used, differed with each wave. The assumption of random attrition from the panel seems well
founded. Changes found from June to October to November in
media use, perceptions of issues, and so forth are best regarded as "true" changes, not methodological artifacts—er-
rors built in by the study method. The panel design's advantage
of providing data about changes over time emerged intact in
Charlotte during 1972.

Content Analysis

In addition to the panel survey, the study employed content
analysis to determine the actual political content of the Charlotte Observer and the content of the television network
evening broadcasts each day the survey was in the field.
Agenda-setting, of course, asserts that over time there will be a
match up between the political stories and issues emphasized
by news media and the issues cited as important by voters.

Table A–2

Sample	June (N=421)	October (N=271)	November (N=254)
Sex and race			
White males	30.7%	30.6%	30.3%
White females	52.2	50.4	50.8
Black males	6.2	7.5	7.5
Black females	10.1	10.7	10.6
Missing data	0.7	0.8	0.8
Political party			
Democrat	72.0	70.2	70.1
Republican	24.2	26.2	26.4
American	3.0	2.8	2.8
Indep., other, or missing data	0.7	0.8	0.8
Age			
17–30	25.3	21.0	20.9
31–40	18.8	18.7	19.7
41–50	21.5	24.2	24.4
51–60	17.8	20.2	20.0
61–70	9.7	9.1	9.1
71 up	6.9	6.0	5.9
Missing data	0.7	0.8	0.8
Education			
0–8	5.9	7.1	7.1
Some high school	9.9	9.9	9.8
High school graduate	26.7	25.0	25.2
Technical or some college	34.7	34.1	34.6
College graduate	22.5	23.8	23.2
Missing data	0.2	0	0
Income			
less than $5000	11.4	12.3	12.2
$5000–10,000	34.4	30.6	31.1
$10,000 up	48.3	50.0	49.6
Missing data	5.9	7.1	7.1

But what is the political content? Voters make choices on the basis of all kinds of issues, including very broad policy questions (war policy) to highly personal issues ("my kid is not safe in school"). Because there are no "natural" boundaries on the kinds of issues all voters *may* find relevant, researchers necessarily have to impose boundaries.

For many issues (Vietnam, the economy, and governmental corruption in 1972), the decision was not difficult. It was more difficult, however, to anticipate just how important minor issues would be to either voters or media. Also some issues might be emphasized far more heavily or lightly, than could have been anticipated early in the campaign. Governmental corruption, for which Watergate became a euphemism, was that kind of issue in 1972.[2]

The "Official Agenda"

Because of the need to focus on issues crucial to both media and voters, the Charlotte study selected seven issues to constitute an "official agenda" for the correlations reported in this book. These issues included four public news areas: (1) Vietnam; (2) American relationships with Russia and Red China as Mr. Nixon worked to open and strengthen what is now called détente; (3) mal-administration in governmental operations (Watergate); and (4) the environment.

Also included, however, were three news-issue areas which were closer to home and more personal for many voters. These were: (5) the economy; (6) drugs; and (7) school busing, an important issue in Charlotte during this period as the city's school system attempted to achieve an acceptable level of integration.

Data Gathering

The national evening news broadcasts of ABC, CBS, and NBC were monitored during the three-week period the June survey was in the field and again for the two-week period during October when the voter panel was interviewed a second time.

Because these were national news broadcasts, they were monitored in Chapel Hill rather than in Charlotte. University of North Carolina students viewed and coded each broadcast. Television news is ephemeral; thus it has to be viewed at the time it is presented unless the researcher has expensive taping equipment available. Coders performed a "dry run" before the actual study coding.

The same kind of training was carried out for two student research assistants who content-analyzed the political news content of the Charlotte *Observer*, Charlotte's leading newspaper. These coders analyzed the political content of the *Observer* for all days in June and October when the voter panel was being interviewed. Using a "constructed week" sampling technique, they also content-analyzed the *Observer* for political content for all other months of 1972.[3]

Reliability is crucial in content analysis. After three training sessions, the coding reliability (i.e., agreement) achieved by the two coders of the content of the *Observer* was +.87 for the entire period. A reliability figure was also computed for the two television coders for the week each viewed the same network. Reliability figures were acceptable, never falling below .75.

The Research Site

Finally, a brief description of the research site, Charlotte, North Carolina, is necessary. Is this a unique case study of one community or can the findings be cautiously extended to other communities?

Two principal criteria were in mind when we selected a site for studying voters and the press during the 1972 presidential election. First, in order to clearly specify the influence of the mass media, we sought a community with an isolated media system. In large metropolitan areas like New York, Chicago, and Los Angeles, there are literally dozens of media voices, each a bit different from the others. Under such circumstances, it is difficult to ascertain to which media voice(s) the voters are responding. But in a community like Charlotte, the two local newspapers plus the NBC and CBS television outlets account for the vast majority of political mass communication received by the voters.

The morning Charlotte *Observer*, North Carolina's largest newspaper, has a daily circulation of 168,000 and Sunday circulation of 217,000. It is a member of the Knight-Ridder group which totals some 30 daily newspapers throughout the United States, including the Detroit *Free Press*, Miami *Herald*, and Philadelphia *Inquirer*.

The *Observer*, which tends to be independent or Democratic in editorial direction, circulates heavily within 18 North and South Carolina counties and is a regional and state newspaper while the afternoon Charlotte *News*, also owned by Knight-Ridder, circulates heavily within Charlotte and Mecklenburg County with its daily circulation of 60,000. The *Observer* maintains news bureaus in the capitals of both North Carolina (Raleigh) and South Carolina (Columbia) and fully covers politics of both states.

One recent survey showed that 63 percent of Charlotte adults read the *Observer* each day while 79 percent or nearly eight of every ten adults, read it on Sunday. One of every three Charlotte adults read the afternoon Charlotte *News*.[4] Charlotte voters also have access to all three networks. The major stations with their percentage of viewing audience earned was shown by the same survey to be the following: WBT (CBS), 32 percent; WSOC (NBC), 22 percent; and WCCB (ABC), 12 percent. All these news outlets devoted heavy attention to the 1972 presidential campaign, and it is feasible to compare voters' thoughts with the specific mass media content they use to obtain evidence about political influence.

We also sought to trace this influence process among a "typical" American population; that is, an increasingly urban group with a substantial number of young, mobile people. In short, we sought a microcosm approximating some of the major trends in American society nationally.

Charlotte is a growing, changing city. In 1960, the Census counted 272,111 people in Charlotte-Mecklenburg. By 1970 the population had increased 30 percent to 354,777. Incomes have been growing too. In 1960 the Effective Buying Income Per Household, that is, the money people actually have to spend, was $7,538. By 1973, it had increased to $14,314—almost double.

Perhaps reflecting both increasing personal incomes plus the general Southern drift toward the Republican Party in presidential voting, Charlotte consistently has leaned toward Republican candidates. Only Democratic Presidents Truman and Johnson managed to beat their opposition during the last seven presidential elections in Mecklenburg County which Charlotte dominates. President Nixon fairly trounced Senator McGovern in 1972. On occasion, Charlotte voters have shown considerable support for third party candidates. On the other hand, except for 1960 when they supported Nixon, Charlotte voters have always picked winners, indicating perhaps the "typicalness" of these voters to those in the nation (see Table A–3).

Increasingly, Charlotte is a community of apartments rather than one-family homes. In 1960 only 15,000 persons lived in apartments, but by 1974, apartment dwellers had increased almost five times. Approximately 30 percent of the people in Charlotte-Mecklenburg now live in apartments.

Charlotte is more and more becoming a transient city. Between 1965 and 1970, 64,703 people over age five moved into Mecklenburg County. Some of these in-migrants, as the U.S. Census Bureau calls them, came from nearby North and South Carolina towns. Most of these were young people who moved to the city to work in Charlotte's offices and industrial parks, and live in Charlotte's many apartments. Another group might be considered the big-time migrants or corporate gypsies, the young and middle-aged executives and their families who are employed by national companies.

Table A-3 Mecklenburg County Presidential Votes, 1948–1972*

Years	% Votes for			Total Votes
	Democrat	Republican	Other	
1972 (McGovern/Nixon/Schmitz)	30%	68%	2%	113,176
1968 (Humphrey/Nixon/Wallace)	29%	52%	19%	107,497
1964 (Johnson/Goldwater)	52%	48%	—	96,171
1960 (Kennedy/Nixon)	45%	55%	—	87,612
1956 (Stevenson/Eisenhower)	38%	62%	—	71,696
1952 (Stevenson/Eisenhower)	43%	57%	—	77,378
1948 (Truman/Dewey/Wallace/ Thurmond)	43%	35%	22%	33,185

*These percentages are based upon data taken from the North Carolina Manual.

Vance Packard refers to a 1970 series of Wall Street *Journal* articles on how various businessmen lived. "One particularly fascinating account," Packard says, "was about a family in Charlotte, North Carolina, the city that has become the branch office hub of the Carolinas for many national corporations."

The article was headlined, "The Jensen's Like Life in Charlotte, But They Won't Be There Long . . . As Corporate Gypsies, They Focus on Job, Avoid Involvement in the Community."

"Mr. Jensen," the article went on to say, "was a man on the move and would probably be offered another job in another city within a year or two. For him and his wife . . . Charlotte was little more than the waystation on the road to business success. That means they can't get to know their neighbors too well, can't become deeply involved in civic affairs, and can't grow too fond of this city."[5]

Annually, 10,000 people like the Jensens move into Mecklenburg. Charlotte is plagued with another variety of transience too: the Monday-morning-get-in-your-car-with-your-briefcase-blues. Because Charlotte is the district office of a great many companies operating in the two Carolinas, approximately 10,000 salespeople leave Charlotte every Monday morning to make the rounds of branch and local offices. The same 10,000 return to Charlotte every Friday afternoon. Charlotte thus shares many of the nation's contemporary social characteristics.

NOTES

[1] Maxwell E. McCombs and Donald L. Shaw, "The Agenda-Setting Function of Mass Media," *Public Opinion Quarterly*, 36:176–87 (Summer 1972).

[2] David Weaver, Maxwell McCombs and Charles Spellman, "Watergate and the Media: A Case Study of Agenda-Setting," *American Politics Quarterly*, 3:458–72 (October 1975).

[3] Robert L. Jones and Roy E. Carter Jr., "Some Procedures for Estimating 'News Hole' in Content Analysis," *Public Opinion Quarterly*, 23:399–403 (Fall 1959).

[4] Knight Publishing Company, *1974 Financial Survey of Mecklenburg County* (Charlotte, September, 1974). The telephone survey was based upon 500 interviews.

[5] See Vance Packard, *A Nation of Strangers* (New York: David McKay, 1972), pp. 258–59.

*

Questionnaire

Questionnaire used in June Wave

Hello, I'm _____. The University of North Caro-
lina at Chapel Hill is conducting a public opinion survey among
registered voters here in Charlotte. Is (name of respondent) at
home?

Your name was selected from the voter list to be interviewed. We want to obtain your opinions on a number of
things. Of course, your answers will be confidential and the
questions take only about twenty minutes.

1. First, what are you most concerned about these days?

Why is that?

(If no national issue mentioned) What about national problems? Which of them are you most concerned about?

2. Would you say you have about as much information as you need to understand these issues?

    ____Yes (go to 2a)
    ____No (go to 2b)

    2a. Do you feel newspapers and television pay *too* much attention to some things?

        ____Yes. What in particular?_____(go to 3)
        ____No (go to 3)
        ____Don't know (go to 3)

    2b. What would you do to learn more about _____?

3. How often do you discuss _____ with others?
    ____Never
    ____Only occasionally
    ____Several times a week
    ____Everyday/nearly everyday

4. How much do you use a *newspaper* for news about political candidates and issues?

    ____A great deal
    ____Some
    ____Very little
    ____Not at all (skip to 5)

    What newspaper is that?

How often do you read this newspaper?

____Only occasionally
____Several times a week
____Everyday/nearly everyday

5.   How much do you use *television* for news about political candidates and issues?

____A great deal
____Some
____Very little
____Not at all (skip to 5b)

  5a. What television news shows do you watch?

     How often do you watch the news on television?
     ____Only occasionally
     ____Several times a week
     ____Everyday/nearly everyday

  5b. How many hours did you happen to watch TV last night?

What is your favorite TV program?

What other programs during the week do you try not to miss?

6.   Do you happen to subscribe to a news magazine?

____No
____Yes   Which one?

7. In general, how often would you say you discuss politics?

_____Almost daily
_____Once or twice a week
_____Just occasionally
_____Never (Go to Question 10)

8. Who do you most often talk with about politics?

_____Family
_____Friends
_____People at work
_____Others_____

9. People take many different roles when talking about politics. Which of the following statements would you say best describes you when you discuss politics?

(HAND RESPONDENT CARD, READ RESPONSES ALOUD AS THEY READ CARD. ONE RESPONSE ONLY.)

_____Even though I may have strong opinions, I usually just listen.
_____I listen a lot, but once in a while I express my opinions.
_____I take an equal share in conversations.
_____I have definite ideas and try to convince others.

Here are some statements about politics. I'd like you to choose from this card the number which indicates how much you agree or disagree with each statement. As you can see, 1 is agree strongly, 2 is agree somewhat, 3 is disagree somewhat, and 4 is disagree strongly.

(HAND RESPONDENT CARD, READ RESPONSES ALOUD AS HE READS CARD, THEN READ QUESTIONS.)

10. I don't think public officials care much what people like me think.

   1 2 3 4

11. The way people vote is the main thing that decides how things are run in this country.

   1 2 3 4

12. Voting is the only way that people like me can have any say about how government runs things.

   1 2 3 4

13. People like me don't have any say about what the government does.

   1 2 3 4

14. Sometimes politics and government seem so complicated that a person like me can't really understand what's going on.

   1 2 3 4

15. People usually register as a party member, Democrat or Republican. Do you consider yourself a *very strong* or *not very strong* party member?

   ____Strong
   ____Not very strong

16. Different people are concerned with very different things. I'm going to show you some cards listing various issues or problems. Each card names two. As I show you each card, tell me which of the two you are more concerned about.

1. Vietnam   Busing

2. Cost of living/unemployment   Pollution

3. Drugs   Relations with Russia/Red China

4. Vietnam   Cost of living/unemployment

5. Busing   Cost of living/unemployment

6. Pollution   Relations with Russia/Red China

7. Drugs   Busing

8. Pollution   Vietnam

9. Cost of living/unemployment   Relations with Russia/Red China

10. Busing   Pollution

11. Drugs   Cost of living/unemployment

12. Vietnam   Relations with Russia/Red China

13. Drugs   Pollution

14. Drugs   Vietnam

15. Busing   Relations with Russia/Red China

17. Do you belong to any groups or organizations to which any of these issues is important?

____Yes
____No

(If yes) What is its name?

Which issues is it concerned with?

18. How interested would you say you are in following the presidential campaign this year?

____Very interested
____Somewhat interested
____Not at all interested

19. Which candidate do you like best for President—or haven't you decided yet?

(If not undecided) Right now, how strongly would you say you feel about your choice?

____Very strongly
____Fairly strongly
____Not at all strongly

20. How much do you care who wins the presidential election in November?

____A great deal
____Somewhat
____Not at all

Now, a few questions about yourself.

21. How far did you go in school?

____0–8 years
____Some high school
____High school graduate
____Technical training/some college
____College graduate

22. Looking at this card, would you tell me what group your family's income was in last year? (HAND RESPONDENT CARD, READ RESPONSES ALOUD AS HE READS CARD.)

   A.   Less than $5,000
   B. $5,000–$10,000
   C.   Over $10,000

23. Here's a card listing some of the last few presidential elections and who was running. Would you take a look at this card and let me know which candidate you voted for if you happened to vote in that election.

   HAND RESPONDENT CARD, READ RESPONSES ALOUD.

1968	Nixon	1960	Kennedy
	Wallace		Nixon
	Humphrey		
		1956	Eisenhower
1964	Johnson		Stevenson
	Goldwater		

   _____

   Respondent's name (please print)

   _____

   Interviewer (sign)

   _____

   _____Observer
          (day of week)

   _____News
          (day of week)

Page	*Heading*	*Page*	*Heading*

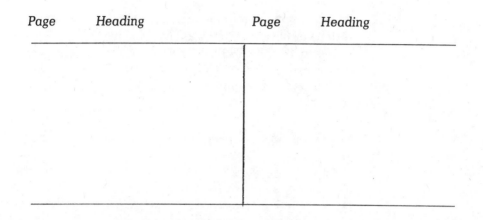

Questionnaire used in October Wave

Hello, I'm _____ from the University of North Carolina survey. Your comments on our questions in June were extremely helpful in understanding this presidential campaign. So we are interviewing a small number of people a second time. Most of the questions are new, but a few are repeats so we can see the changes going on.

1.   First, what are *you* most concerned about these days?

Why is that?

(If no national issue mentioned) What about national problems? Which of them are you most concerned about?

2. Here are some other statements people have made about various issues. For each statement tell me the number on this card (HAND RESPONDENT CARD) that best represents your opinion. As you can see, 1 is strongly disagree, 2 is disagree, 3 is not sure, 4 is agree, and 5 is strongly agree.

    Busing is good for our school children.

    1 2 3 4 5

    The United States should keep at least a few troops in South Vietnam for several more years.

    1 2 3 4 5

    Pollution is not a serious problem.

    1 2 3 4 5

    We should improve our relations with Russia and Red China.

    1 2 3 4 5

    The United States is in good economic condition.

    1 2 3 4 5

    Drugs are no longer a serious problem.

    1 2 3 4 5

3. Which candidate do you like best for President—or haven't you decided yet?

(If decided) Right now, how strongly would you say you feel about your choice?

____Very strongly
____Fairly strongly
____Not at all strongly

4. How do you think your closest friends are going to vote?

____All Democratic
____Mostly Democratic
____About half Democratic and about half Republican
____Mostly Republican
____All Republican
____Don't know

5. What about your family?

____All Democratic
____Mostly Democratic
____About half Democratic and about half Republican
____Mostly Republican
____All Republican
____Don't know

6. Suppose there was someone who was undecided about who to vote for in the presidential election. What would you tell that person about each candidate? First, what would you tell him about President Nixon?

What would you tell him about Senator McGovern?

7. Who do you most often talk with about politics?

    ____Family
    ____Friends
    ____People at work
    ____Others _____

8. In general, how often would you say you discuss politics?

    ____Almost daily
    ____Once or twice a week
    ____Just occasionally
    ____Never

9. How much do you use a *newspaper* for news about political candidates and issues?

    ____A great deal
    ____Some
    ____Very little
    ____Not at all

10. How much do you use *television* for news about political candidates and issues?

    ____A great deal
    ____Some
    ____Very little
    ____Not at all (skip to 11)

    What television news shows do you watch?

11. The two presidential candidates have had advertising on
     television lately. About how many commercials do you re-
     call seeing for President Nixon?

     ___Many
     ___Only a few
     ___None (skip to 12)

     What are some of the things you remember from those
     ads?

12. About how many commercials do you recall seeing for
     Senator McGovern?

     ___Many
     ___Only a few
     ___None (skip to 13)

     What are some of the things you remember from those
     ads?

13. Here are some names of people and things that have been
     in the news on and off. Can you happen to tell me who or
     what they are?

     Viet Cong

     marijuana

Environmental Protection Agency

racial balance in the schools

President Thieu

methadone

14. So far in this year's election campaign, have you done any of these, or not?

Yes   No

___ ___   Go door-to-door for a political candidate or group?

___ ___   Spend time working for a political candidate or group—doing things like telephoning, writing letters or addressing envelopes, or similar campaign activities?

___ ___   Contribute money to (or buy tickets to help) a political candidate or group?

___ ___   Wear a campaign button or put a bumper sticker on your car?

___ ___   Write or telephone a political candidate or group, or a newspaper editor?

___ ___   Attend a political meeting, rally or speech?

Here are some statements about politics. I'd like you to choose from this card the number which indicates how much you agree or disagree with each statement. As you can see, 1 is agree strongly, 2 is agree somewhat, 3 is disagree somewhat, and 4 is disagree strongly.

(HAND REPONDENT CARD, READ RESPONSES ALOUD AS HE READS CARD, THEN READ QUESTIONS.)

15. It isn't so important to vote when you know your party doesn't have a chance to win.

    1   2   3   4

16. A good many local elections aren't important enough to bother with.

    1   2   3   4

17. So many other people vote in the national elections that it doesn't matter much to me whether I vote or not.

    1   2   3   4

18. If a person doesn't care how an election comes out he shouldn't vote in it.

    1   2   3   4

19. Thinking about the first issue you mentioned to me, would you say you have about as much information as you need to understand it?

    ____Yes
    ____No (go to 20)

Do you feel newspapers and television are paying *too* much attention to some things?

____Yes.   What in particular?

____No
____Don't know

20. For each of these statements about issues in the campaign, tell me how you think Nixon and McGovern would answer. Let's use the same numbers we used a few minutes ago. (HAND RESPONDENT CARD.)

Busing is good for our school children.

McGovern: 1   2   3   4   5   DK

Nixon: 1   2   3   4   5   DK

The United States should keep at least a few troops in South Vietnam for several more years.

McGovern: 1   2   3   4   5   DK

Nixon   1   2   3   4   5   DK

Pollution is not a serious problem.

McGovern: 1   2   3   4   5   DK

Nixon: 1   2   3   4   5   DK

We should improve our relations with Russia and Red China.

McGovern: 1 2 3 4 5   DK

Nixon: 1 2 3 4 5   DK

The United States is in good economic condition.

McGovern: 1 2 3 4 5   DK

Nixon: 1 2 3 4 5   DK

Drugs are no longer a serious problem.

McGovern: 1 2 3 4 5   DK

Nixon: 1 2 3 4 5   DK

21. During the campaign, there has been some news and discussion about the Watergate wiretapping incident. Do you happen to have seen or heard anything about it?

No/Don't know ____ (go to Question 22)
Yes ____

As you understand it, what is the incident all about?

So far as you personally feel, how important is this incident in the campaign?

____Very important
____Somewhat important
____Not important at all

22. Different people are concerned with very different things.
    I'm going to show you some cards listing various issues or
    problems. Each card names two. As I show you each card,
    tell me which of the two you are more concerned about.

    1. Vietnam   Busing

    2. Cost of living/unemployment   Pollution

    3. Drugs   Relations with Russia/Red China

    4. Vietnam   Cost of living/unemployment

    5. Busing   Cost of living/unemployment

    6. Pollution   Relations with Russia/Red China

    7. Drugs   Busing

    8. Pollution   Vietnam

    9. Cost of living/unemployment   Relations with
        Russia/Red China

    10. Busing   Pollution

    11. Drugs   Cost of living/unemployment

    12. Vietnam   Relations with Russia/Red China

    13. Drugs   Pollution

    14. Drugs   Vietnam

    15. Busing   Relations with Russia/Red China

_____

_____Observer   ____ Does not read
     (day of week)   newspaper

_____News   ____ Did not read today's
     (day of week)   paper

Page	*Heading*	*Page*	*Heading*

Office Use Only

_____

Date

_____

Respondent's name (please print)

Precinct_____

June serial number_____

How comfortable did you feel in this interview?

very uncomfortable / ___/ ___/ ___/ ___/ ___/ very comfortable

How cooperative did you find the respondent?

very cooperative / ___/ ___/ ___/ ___/ ___/ not at all cooperative

How would you rate the quality of the information obtained from the respondent?

very good / ___/ ___/ ___/ ___/ ___/ very poor

Interviewer_____

Questionnaire used for the November Telephone Wave

Hello, this is the North Carolina Poll at the University of North Carolina. We'd like to ask you three quick questions about the November 7th election.

1. First, did you happen to vote in the election?

    ____No   What was the main reason you didn't get to vote?

    ____Yes

    Which presidential candidate did you vote for?

    ____Nixon
    ____McGovern

    For U.S. Senator, did you vote for Galifinakis or Helms?

    ____Galifinakis
    ____Helms

2. In the presidential election what was the most important issue for you?

    Thank you

    _____   _____
    Respondent's name   Interviewer

    *

Bibliography

"Agenda-setting" research is the code name for a new group of studies in the relatively young field of mass communications research which basically focuses upon the amount of audience learning which takes place as a result of exposure to the press. How much do we learn from the enormous amounts of time we collectively spend with the mass press? It is a far more complicated question than it may seem.

Serious exposure to press news does not always result in very significant "learning" (at least that we can measure) while we may unconsciously be learning about many aspects of life—for example, crime—by our viewing of television entertainment programs. Agenda-setting research follows up the assertion astutely made in the 1920s by journalist-scholar Walter Lippmann that the press sketches in our "unseen environment." If so, how does it do that? During the same period, Hitler also took notice of the press and argued that masses of people can be manipulated by repetitious treatment of certain themes in the press. Despite his successful (for a time) career, can it be that simple?

Political scientist Bernard Cohen argues that the press may not be able to tell us what to think, but it does seem to have the power to determine what we will think about. If so, that is enormous power and McCombs and Shaw in 1972 (see follow-ing citations) attempted one of the first empirical tests of this relationship between press content and audience learning.

Since then, students of Shaw and McCombs and other scholars and their students have conducted additional re-search to replicate the recent findings of McCombs and Shaw (and of course Lippmann, Cohen, and many others who have postulated a press→audience learning relationship) or to learn the conditions under which learning does or does not take place from the press. By 1977 many studies had been com-pleted, a few of them based upon the Charlotte data while others were based upon completely new data.

Many recent studies have established that, in fact, there is a relationship between press content and audience learning but the more difficult and intriguing research questions have to do with locating the key variables from the multitude potentially involved and tracing out their separate influence.

The bibliography which follows shows that one group of studies has attempted to establish the contingent conditions under which audience learning is most likely to take place. For example, are those in the audience who simply have more ex-posure to the press more likely to learn from it? Are those with a greater "need for orientation"—those with more mental room to learn—more likely to learn? Likewise, is there a dif-ference in learning according to how you plan to use the infor-mation, *if* you plan to "use" it at all?

Other studies have concentrated upon measuring effects across time, directly addressing the tough chicken-egg ques-tion of which comes first, media content or audience interest. Various media are also contrasted for their possible different effects in some studies while still other studies have con-centrated upon studying which parts of messages—which at-tributes—are learned. Still other studies have contrasted dif-ferent types of content (such as advertising) or looked at dif-ferent analysis levels (such as state versus national).

The selective literature which follows sorts many studies by these basic subgroups. Not all are agenda-setting studies by any means. Some studies fall into more than one category and other studies could be listed. This list provides a start. Agenda-setting research is a subfield of the larger area of mass communication research which is inching toward a more theoretical understanding of press→audience relationships. That should be evident from this bibliography. Slowly and surely, however, the research is filling in the (still large) conceptual and empirical holes in the agenda-setting research literature.

Because agenda-setting research is young, much of the literature is still in the form of research papers, which usually can be obtained by writing to the authors of these papers; nevertheless the article literature is growing.

General

Atkin, C. K.; Bowen, L.; Nayman, O. B.; and Sheinkopf, K. C. "Quality versus Quantity in Televised Political Ads." *Public Opinion Quarterly* 37 (Summer 1973): 209–24.

Beardsley, P. L. "The Methodology of the Electoral Analysis: Models and Measurement." In *Explaining the Vote: Presidential Choices in the Nation and States, 1968,* edited by D. M. Kovenock and J. W. Prothro. Chapel Hill: Institute for Research in Social Science, 1973.

Becker, L.; McCombs, M.; and McLeod, J. "The Development of Political Cognitions." In *Political Communication,* edited by S. H. Chaffee. Sage Annual Reviews of Communication Research, vol. 4. Beverly Hills, CA: Sage, 1975.

Bernstein, C., and Woodward, B. *All The President's Men.* New York: Warner, 1975.

Blumler, J. G., and McQuail, D. *Television in Politics: Its Uses and Influence.* Chicago: University of Chicago Press, 1969.

Breed, W. "Social Control in the Newsroom: A Functional Analysis." *Social Forces* 33 (May 1955):326–35.

Burnham, W. D. "The End of American Party Politics." *Transaction* 7 (December 1969):12–22.

Campbell, A., et al. *The American Voter*. New York: John Wiley and Sons, 1960.

Campbell, A.; Converse, P. E.; Miller, W. E.; and Stokes, D. E. *Elections and the Political Order*. New York: John Wiley and Sons, 1966.

Campbell, A.; Gurin, G.; and Miller, W. E. *The Voter Decides*. Evanston, IL: Row, Peterson and Co., 1954.

Campbell, A., and Converse, P. E., eds. *The Human Meaning of Social Change*. New York: Russell Sage, 1972.

Cantril, H. *The Invasion From Mars*. Princeton, NJ: Princeton University Press, 1940; New York: Harper, 1966.

Chaffee, S. H.; Ward, L. S.; and Tipton, L. P. "Mass Communication and Political Socialization." *Journalism Quarterly* 47 (Winter 1970): 647–59, 666.

Cobb, R. W., and Elder, C. D. *Participation in American Politics: The Dynamics of Agenda-Building*. Boston: Allyn and Bacon, 1972.

Crouse, T. *The Boys on the Bus*. New York: Ballantine, 1972.

DeFleur, M. L. *Theories of Mass Communication*. 2d ed. New York: McKay, 1970.

Dervin, B., and Greenberg, B. S. "The Communication Environment of the Urban Poor." In *Current Perspectives in Mass Communications Research*, edited by F. G. Kline and P. Tichenor, pp. 195–233. Beverly Hills, CA: Sage Publications, 1972.

DeVries, W., and Tarrance, V. L., Jr. *The Ticket Splitter: A New Force in American Politics*. Grand Rapids, MI: William B. Eerdmans, 1972.

Dreyer, E. C. "Media Use and Electoral Choices: Some Political Consequences of Information Exposure." *Public Opinion Quarterly* 35 (Winter 1971–72):544–53.

Festinger, L. *A Theory of Cognitive Dissonance.* Stanford: Stanford University Press, 1957.

Hiebert, R.; Jones, R.; Lorenz, J.; and Lotito, E., eds. *The Political Image Merchants: Strategies in the New Politics.* Washington, DC: Acropolis Books, 1971.

Hitler, A. *Mein Kampf.* New York: Reynal and Hitchcock, 1939. First published in 1925.

Jones, R. L., and Carter, R. E., Jr. "Some Procedures for Estimating 'News Hole' in Content Analysis." *Public Opinion Quarterly* 23 (Fall 1959):399–400.

Katz, E., et al. "Uses and Gratifications Research." *Public Opinion Quarterly* 38 (Winter 1973–74):509–21.

Katz, E., and Lazarsfeld, P. F. *Personal Influence.* Glencoe, IL: The Free Press, 1955.

Kelley, S. *Professional Public Relations and Political Power.* Baltimore: The Johns Hopkins University Press, 1956.

Key, V. O., Jr. *The Responsible Electorate.* New York: Vintage, 1966.

Klapper, J. *The Effects of Mass Communication.* Glencoe, IL: The Free Press, 1960.

Kovenock, D. M., and Prothro, J. W., eds. *Explaining the Vote: Presidential Choices in the Nation and States, 1968.* Chapel Hill: Institute for Research in Social Science, 1973.

Lane, R. E. "Alienation, Protest and Rootless Politics in the Seventies." In *The Political Image Merchants: Strategies in the New Politics,* edited by R. Hiebert et al, pp. 273–300. Washington, DC: Acropolis Books, 1971.

Lang, K., and Lang, G. E. *Politics and Television.* Chicago: Quadrangle, 1968.

Lasswell, H. "The Structure and Function of Communication in Society." In *Mass Communications,* edited by W. Schramm, pp. 117–130. Urbana: University of Illinois Press, 1960.

Lazarsfeld, P.; Berelson, B.; and Gaudet, H. *The People's Choice*. New York: Columbia University Press, 1948.

Lazarsfeld, P. F., and Merton, R. K. "Mass Communication, Popular Taste and Organized Social Action." In *The Communication of Ideas*, edited by L. Bryson, pp. 95–118. New York: Institute for Religious and Social Studies, 1948.

Lippmann, W. *Public Opinion*. New York: Macmillan, 1922.

McCombs, M. E. "Mass Communication in Political Campaigns: Information, Gratification, and Persuasion." In *Current Perspectives in Mass Communication Research*, edited by F. G. Kline and P. J. Tichenor, pp. 169–194. Beverly Hills, CA: Sage Publications, 1972.

_____. "Mass Media in the Marketplace." *Journalism Monographs*, no. 24 (August 1972).

McCombs, M. E., and Shaw, D. L. "Structuring the 'Unseen Environment.' " *Journal of Communication* 26 (Spring 1976):18–22.

McGinniss, J. *The Selling of the President 1968*. New York: Trident Press, 1969.

McLuhan, M. *Understanding Media*. New York: McGraw-Hill, 1964.

May, E. R., and Fraser, J., eds. *Campaign '72: The Managers Speak*. Cambridge: Harvard University Press, 1973.

Miller, G. A. "The Magic Number Seven, Plus or Minus Two: Some Limits on Our Capacity for Processing Information." *Psychological Review* 63 (March 1956):81–97.

Mueller, J. E. "Choosing Among 133 Candidates." *Public Opinion Quarterly* 34 (Fall 1970):395–402.

National Institute of Mental Health. *Television and Growing Up: The Impact of Televised Violence, A Report to the Surgeon General of Public Health Service from Surgeon General's Scientific Advisory Committee on Television and Social Behavior*. Washington, DC: Government Printing Office, 1972.

Nixon, R. B., and Ward, J. "Trends in Newspaper Ownership and Inter-Media Competition." *Journalism Quarterly* 38 (Winter 1961):3–14.

Packard, V. *A Nation of Strangers.* New York: David McKay, 1972.

Paletz, D. L.; Reichert, P.; and McIntyre, B. "How the Media Support Local Governmental Authority." *Public Opinion Quarterly* 35 (Spring 1971):80–92.

Parker, E. B. "Technological Change and the Mass Media." In *Handbook of Communication*, edited by I. de Sola Pool and W. Schramm, pp. 619–45. Chicago: Rand McNally, 1973.

Penrose, J., et al. "The Newspaper Nonreader 10 Years Later: A Partial Replication of Westley-Severin." *Journalism Quarterly* 51 (Winter 1974):631–38.

Perry, J. M. *Us & Them: How the Press Covered the 1972 Election.* New York: Clarkson N. Potter, 1973.

Phillips, D. W. "International and World Public Opinion." In *Handbook of Communication*, edited by I. de Sola Pool and W. Schramm, pp. 871–86. Chicago: Rand McNally, 1973.

Pye, L. W. "Models of Traditional, Transitional, and Modern Communication Systems." In *Communications and Political Development*, edited by L. W. Pye, pp. 24–29. Princeton, NJ: Princeton University Press, 1963.

RePass, D. E. "Issue Salience and Party Choice." *American Political Science Review* 65 (June 1971):389–400.

Report of the National Advisory Commission on Civil Disorders. New York: Bantam Books, 1968.

Reston, J. B. *The Artillery of the Press.* New York: Harper and Row, 1967.

Rivers, W. L. *The Adversaries: Politics and the Press.* Boston: Beacon Press, 1970.

Rogers, R. *How Russians Read Their Press: Patterns of Selection in Pravda and Izvestia.* Cambridge, MA: Center for International Studies, 1968.

Schramm, W. "The Effects of Mass Communications: A Review." *Journalism Quarterly* 26 (December 1949):397–409.

Shaw, D. L. "Surveillance vs. Constraint: Press Coverage of a Social Issue." *Journalism Quarterly* 46 (Winter 1969):707–12.

Siebert, F.; Peterson, T.; and Schramm, W. *Four Theories of the Press.* Urbana: University of Illinois Press, 1956.

Surlin, S. H., and Gordon, T. F. "Selective Exposure and Retention of Political Advertising: A Regional Comparison." Paper presented to the International Communication Association, New Orleans, LA, 1974.

Tolman, E. C. *Purposive Behavior in Animals and Men.* New York: Appleton-Century, 1932.

Trenaman, J., and McQuail, D. *Television and the Political Image.* London: Methuen, 1961.

Westley, B. H., and Barrow, L. "An Investigation of News Seeking Behavior." *Journalism Quarterly* 36 (Fall 1959):431–438.

Westley, B. H., and Severin, W. J. "A Profile of the Daily Newspaper Non-Reader." *Journalism Quarterly,* 41 (Winter 1964):45–50, 156.

White, D. M. "The 'Gate Keeper': A Case Study in Selection of News." *Journalism Quarterly* 27 (Fall 1950):83–90.

White, T. *The Making of the President 1972.* New York: Bantam, 1973.

Wiebe, G. D. "Mass Media and Man's Relationship to His Environment." *Journalism Quarterly* 50 (Autumn 1973):426–32, 446.

Agenda-Setting: "Main Effect"*

Arnold, D., and Gold, D. "The Facilitation Effect of Social Environment." *Public Opinion Quarterly* 28 (Fall 1964):513–16.

Becker, L. B., and McLeod, J. M. "Political Consequences of Agenda-Setting." Paper presented to the Conference on the Agenda-Setting Function of the Press, Syracuse University, Syracuse, NY, 1974.

Berelson, B.; Lazarsfeld, P.; and McPhee, W. *Voting*. Chicago: University of Chicago Press, 1954.

Bloj, A. J. "Into the Wild Blue Yonder: Behavioral Implications of Agenda-Setting for Air Travel." In *Studies in Agenda-Setting*, edited by M. McCombs and G. Stone. Syracuse, NY: Newhouse Communication Research Center, Syracuse University, 1976.

Cohen, B. C. *The Press and Foreign Policy*. Princeton, NJ: Princeton University Press, 1963.

DeFleur, M. L., and DeFleur, L. "The Relative Contribution of Television as a Learning Source for Children's Occupational Knowledge." *American Sociological Review* 32 (October 1967):777–89.

Donohue, G. A.; Tichenor, P. J.; and Olien, C. N. "Mass Media and the Knowledge Gap: A Hypothesis Reconsidered." *Communication Research* 2 (January 1975):3–23.

Funkhouser, G. R. "The Issues of the Sixties: An Exploratory Study in the Dynamics of Public Opinion." *Public Opinion Quarterly* 37 (Spring 1975):62–75.

_____. "Trends in Media Coverage of the Issues of the '60s." *Journalism Quarterly* 50 (Autumn 1973):533–38.

Krugman, H. E. "The Impact of Television Advertising: Learning Without Involvement." *Public Opinion Quarterly* 29 (Fall 1965):349–56.

McClure, R. D., and Patterson, T. E. "*The People's Choice* Revisited in the Age of Television." Paper presented at the American Association for Public Opinion Research, Lake George, NY, May, 1974.

McCombs, M. "Working Papers on Agenda-Setting." Chapel Hill: University of North Carolina School of Journalism, July, 1973.

McCombs, M. E., and Shaw, D. L. "The Agenda-Setting Function of Mass Media." *Public Opinion Quarterly* 36 (Summer 1972):176–87.

Meadow, R. G. "Issue Emphasis and Public Opinion: The Media during the 1972 Presidential Campaign." *American Politics Quarterly* 4 (April 1976):177–92.

Shaw, D. L., and Long, C. L. "Voters and Issues: A Study of Media Agenda-Setting in the 1972 Campaign." Report to the National Association of Broadcasters, Chapel Hill, University of North Carolina School of Journalism, January, 1975.

Siune, K., and Borre, O. "Setting the Agenda for a Danish Election." *Journal of Communication* 25 (Winter 1975):65–73.

Stevenson, R. L., and Stiles, S. K. "Agenda Effects of the Presidential Debates." Chapel Hill, University of North Carolina School of Journalism, August, 1977. Mimeographed.

Weaver, D., and Spellman, C. "Watergate and the Media: A Case Study of Agenda-Setting." Paper presented to the International Communication Association, New Orleans, LA, April, 1974.

Westley, B. H. "What Makes It Change?" *Journal of Communication* 26 (Spring 1976):43–47.

Agenda-Setting: Comparing Media

Agnir, F. "Testing New Approaches to Agenda-Setting: A Replication and Extension." In *Studies in Agenda-Setting,* edited by M. McCombs and G. Stone. Syracuse, NY: Newhouse Communication Research Center, Syracuse University, 1976.

Cohen, A. A. "Radio vs. TV: The Effect of the Medium." *Journal of Communication* 26 (Spring 1976):29–35.

McClure, R. D., and Patterson, T. E. "Agenda-Setting: Comparison of Newspaper and Television Network News." Paper presented to the Conference on the Agenda-Setting Function of the Press, Syracuse University, Syracuse, NY, October, 1974.

_____. "Print vs. Network News." *Journal of Communication* 26 (Spring 1976):23–28.

_____. "Television News and Political Advertising: The Impact of Exposure on Voter Beliefs." *Communication Research* 1 (January 1974):3–31.

_____. "Television News and Voter Behavior in the 1972 Presidential Election." Paper presented to the American Political Science Association, New Orleans, LA, 1973.

McCombs, M. E. and Bowers, T. "Television's Effects on Political Behavior." In *The Fifth Season: How TV Influences the Ways People Behave,* edited by G. Comstock et al. Santa Monica, CA: Rand Corporation, forthcoming.

McCombs, M. E., and Shaw, D. L. "The Agenda-Setting Function of Mass Media." *Public Opinion Quarterly* 36 (Summer 1972):176–87.

McCombs, M. E.; Shaw, D.; and Shaw, E. "The News and Public Response: Three Studies of the Agenda-Setting Power of the Press." Paper presented to the Association for Education in Journalism, Carbondale, IL, 1972.

Mullins, L. M. "Agenda-Setting on the Campus: The Mass Media and Learning of Issue Importance in the '72 Election." Paper presented to the Association for Education in Journalism, Fort Collins, CO, 1973.

Patterson, T. E., and McClure, R. D. *The Unseeing Eye.* New York: Putnam, 1976.

Shaw, D. L. "The 1971 Economic Freeze: From Event to Issue." In "Working Papers on Agenda-Setting," edited by M. McCombs. Chapel Hill: University of North Carolina School of Journalism, July, 1973.

Tipton, L.; Haney, R. D.; and Baseheart, J. B. "Media Agenda-Setting in City and State Election Campaigns." *Journalism Quarterly* 52 (Spring 1975):15–22.

Williams, W. "The Agenda-Setting Function of Newspapers and Public Radio: An Analysis of the Intrapersonal Method." Paper presented to the Speech Communication Association, Houston, TX, 1975.

Agenda-Setting: Effects Across Time

McCombs, M. E.; Becker, L.; and Weaver, D. "Measuring the Cumulative Agenda-Setting Influence of the Mass Media." Paper presented to the Mass Communication Division, Speech Communication Association, Houston, TX, 1975.

McCombs, M. E., and Schulte, H. F. "The Expanding Domain of the Agenda-Setting Function of Mass Communication." Paper presented to the World Association for Public Opinion Research, Montreux, Switzerland, 1975.

Stone, G. "Tracing the Time-Lag in Agenda-Setting." In *Studies in Agenda-Setting*, edited by M. McCombs and G. Stone. Syracuse, NY: Newhouse Communication Research Center, Syracuse University, 1976.

Tipton, L.; Haney, R. D.; and Baseheart, J. B. "Media Agenda-Setting in City and State Election Campaigns." *Journalism Quarterly* 52 (Spring 1975):15–22.

Agenda-Setting: Contingent Conditions

Agnir, F. "Testing New Approaches to Agenda-Setting: A Replication and Extension." In *Studies in Agenda-Setting*, edited by M. McCombs and G. Stone. Syracuse, NY: Newhouse Communication Research Center, Syracuse University, 1976.

Barbič, A. "Participation or Escape?" *Journal of Communication* 26 (Spring 1976):36–42.

Cole, E. B. "Surveillance and Voter Decision-Making: A Dynamic Model of Need for Orientation." Paper presented to the International Communication Association, New Orleans, LA, April, 1974.

McCombs, M. "Editorial Endorsements: A Study of Influence." *Journalism Quarterly* 44 (Autumn 1967):545–48.

McCombs, M. E.; Shaw, D.; and Shaw, E. "The News and Public Response: Three Studies of the Agenda-Setting Power of the Press." Paper presented to the Association for Education in Journalism, Carbondale, IL, 1972.

McCombs, M., and Weaver, D. "Voters' Need for Orientation and Use of Mass Communications." Paper presented to the International Communication Association, Montreal, Canada, April, 1973.

Mullins, L. E. "Agenda-Setting on the Campus: The Mass Media and Learning of Issue Importance in the '72 Election." Paper presented to the Association for Education in Journalism, Fort Collins, CO, 1973.

Shaw, E. F. "Some Interpersonal Dimensions of the Media's Agenda-Setting Function." Paper presented at the Conference on the Agenda-Setting Function of the Press, Syracuse University, Syracuse, NY, October, 1974.

Weaver, D.; McCombs, M. E.; and Spellman, C. "Watergate and the Media: A Case Study of Agenda-Setting." *American Politics Quarterly* 3 (October 1975):458–72.

Agenda-Setting: Intrapersonal vs. Interpersonal Use of the Press Agenda

Agnir, F. "Testing New Approaches to Agenda-Setting: A Replication and Extension." In *Studies in Agenda-Setting,* edited by M. McCombs and G. Stone, Syracuse, NY: Newhouse Communication Research Center, Syracuse University, 1976.

McLeod, J. M.; Becker, L. B.; and Byrnes, J. E. "Another Look at the Agenda-Setting Function of the Press." *Communication Research* 1 (April 1974):131–66.

McCombs, M. E. "A Comparison of Intra-personal and Inter-personal Agenda of Public Issues." Paper presented to the International Communication Association, New Orleans, LA, April, 1974.

Agenda-Setting: Message Attributes

Benton, M., and Frazier, P. J. "The Agenda-Setting Function of the Mass Media at Three Levels of Information-Holding." *Communication Research* 3 (July 1976):261–74.

Cohen, D. "A Report on a Non-Election Agenda-Setting Study." Paper presented to the Association for Education in Journalism, Ottawa, Canada, 1975.

McCombs, M. E., and Bowers, T. "Television's Effects on Political Behavior." In *The Fifth Season: How TV Influences the Ways People Behave,* edited by G. Comstock et al. Santa Monica, CA: Rand Corporation, forthcoming.

McCombs, M. E., and Shaw, D. L. "Progress Report on Agenda-Setting Research." Paper presented to the Association for Education in Journalism, San Diego, CA, 1974.

Sanders, K., and Atwood, E. "Communication Exposure and Electoral Decision Making." Paper presented to the Association for Education in Journalism, Ottawa, Canada, 1975.

Weaver, D. H., and Wilhoit, G. C. "Agenda-Setting for the Media: Determinants of Senatorial News Coverage." Paper presented to the International Communication Association, Chicago, IL, 1975.

Westley, B. H. "What Makes It Change?" *Journal of Communication* 26 (Spring 1976):43–47.

Agenda-Setting: Contrasting Media Content or Levels of Analysis

Benton, M., and Frazier, P. J. "The Agenda-Setting Function of the Mass Media at Three Levels of 'Information Holding.' " *Communication Research* 3 (July 1976):261–74.

Bowers, T. A. "Newspaper Political Advertising and the Agenda-Setting Function." *Journalism Quarterly* 50 (Autumn 1973):552–56.

————. "Political Advertising: Setting the Candidate's Agenda." Paper presented to the Conference on the Agenda-Setting Function of the Press, Syracuse University, Syracuse, NY, October, 1974.

Chaffee, S. H., and Wilson, D. "Media Rich, Media Poor: Two Studies of Diversity in Agenda-Holding." Paper presented to the Association for Education in Journalism, College Park, MD, August, 1976.

Cohen, B. C. *The Press and Foreign Policy.* Princeton, NJ: Princeton University Press, 1963.

Cohen, D. "A Report on a Non-Election Agenda-Setting Study." Paper presented to the Association for Education in Journalism, Ottawa, Canada, 1975.

Gormley, W. T., Jr. "Newspaper Agendas and Political Elites." *Journalism Quarterly* 52 (Summer 1975):304–08.

Martin, S. A. "Youth Unrest on the National Agenda: Studying a Decade of Public Opinion." In *Studies in Agenda-Setting,* edited by M. McCombs and G. Stone. Syracuse, NY: Newhouse Communication Research Center, Syracuse University, 1976.

McClure, R. D., and Patterson, T. E. "Television News and Political Advertising." *Communication Research* 1 (January 1974):3–31.

McCombs, M. E., and Bowers, T. "Television's Effects on Political Behavior." In *The Fifth Season: How TV Influences the*

Ways People Behave, edited by G. Comstock et al. Santa Monica, CA: Rand Corporation, forthcoming.

McCombs, M. E., and Schulte, H. F. "Expanding the Domain of the Agenda-Setting Function of Mass Communication." Paper presented to the World Association for Public Opinion Research, Montreux, Switzerland, 1975.

Mullins, L. E. "Agenda-Setting on the Campus: The Mass Media and Learning of Issue Importance in the '72 Election." Paper presented to the Association for Education in Journalism, Fort Collins, CO, 1973.

_____. "Mass Communication on the Campus: A Descriptive and Causal Analysis of Information-Seeking and Political Behavior During the 1972 Presidential Election." Ph.D. dissertation, University of North Carolina, Chapel Hill, NC, 1974.

Patterson, T. E., and McClure, R. D. "Political Advertising: Voter Reaction." Paper presented to the Annual Meeting of the American Association for Public Opinion Research, Asheville, NC, May, 1973.

Sanders, K., and Atwood, E. "Communication Exposure and Electoral Decision Making." Paper presented to the Association for Education in Journalism, Ottawa, Canada, 1975.

Shaw, D. L., and Bowers, T. A. "Learning from Commercials: The Influence of TV Advertising on the Voter Political Agenda." Paper presented to the Association for Education in Journalism, Fort Collins, CO, August, 1973.

Tipton, L.; Haney, R. D.; and Baseheart, J. B. "Media Agenda-Setting in City and State Election Campaigns." *Journalism Quarterly* 52 (Spring 1975):15–22.

*Many studies listed in these special sections are not agenda-setting studies strictly speaking, but all of them contain important data or arguments dealing with the press→audience relationship. Some studies are listed several times.

Index

†